TALES OF THE

OLD VILLAGERS

Selling homegrown flowers outside the cottage door

TALES OF THE
OLD
VILLAGERS

BRIAN P. MARTIN

DAVID & CHARLES

BY THE SAME AUTHOR

Tales from the Country Pub
Tales of the Old Countrymen
More Tales of the Old Countrymen
Tales of the Old Countrywomen
Tales of the Old Gamekeepers
More Tales of the Old Gamekeepers
Tales of Time and Tide: *Stories of Life on Britain's Coasts*
Birds of Prey of the British Isles
Sporting Birds of Britain and Ireland
The Great Shoots: *Britain's Premier Sporting Estates*

All photographs from personal collections except the following:
Beaford Archive 4, 6, 7, 10–11, 12, 16, 17, 28, 35, 38, 39, 40, 55, 69, 77, 89, 90, 95, 96, 100–1,
102, 103, 106, 129, 138, 139, 156–7, 165, 169, 183, 188, 189, 191; James Ravilious 80, 131, 181

Illustrations by John Paley and Robin Wiggins

A DAVID & CHARLES BOOK

First published in the UK in 1997
First published in paperback in 1999

Copyright © Brian P. Martin 1997, 1999

Brian P. Martin has asserted his right to be identified as author of this work in
accordance with the Copyright, Designs and Patents Act, 1988.

A catalogue record for this book is available from the British Library.

Hardback ISBN 0 7153 0348 1
Paperback ISBN 0 7153 1003 8

Typeset by ABM Typographics Limited Hull
and printed in Great Britain
by Butler & Tanner Ltd
for David & Charles
Brunel House   Newton Abbot   Devon

CONTENTS

Introduction   7

In Good Service · *Margaret Jackson, Housemaid, Buckinghamshire*   14

A Fair Cop · *Frank Perchard, Policeman, East Sussex*   31

Mine Host · *John Sibley, Publican, Dorset*   48

Much to His Credit · *John Gwynne, Shopkeeper, Breconshire*   61

Out of Africa · *Alice Murnane, Dispensing Doctor, County Meath*   72

Beyond Living Memory   82

Ministering to Two Flocks · *The Reverend Fred Pennington,*   86
    Priest and Farmer, Devon

Much More than Rubber Stamps · *Elizabeth Williams and*   110
    Joy Johnson, Postmistresses, Shropshire and Oxfordshire

From Horseback to Helicopter · *Joyce Damerell, District*   122
    Nurse and Midwife, Devon and Wiltshire

Leader of the Community · *John Fairless, Schoolmaster, Ayrshire and*   134
    Peeblesshire

Beyond Living Memory   146

Living off the Fat · *Victor Wilson, Butcher, Staffordshire*   150

A Truly Helping Hand · *Will Jones, Gardener, Shropshire and Lancashire*   159

Master of His Own Muck Heap · *Peter Pearl, Farmer and*   171
    Policeman, Hampshire and Essex

Acknowledgements   188

Index   189

*(above) Something interesting in the grocer's window; (opposite) Gathering sheep prior to dipping,
an operation they hated, and one which often involved the whole family to persuade them into the pens*

INTRODUCTION

According to my dictionary, a village is a 'group of houses etc, larger than hamlet and smaller than town; small municipality with limited corporate powers'. However, most of us have a good idea of what constitutes a village without taking out the measuring tape. It is a place which lurks in the subconscious, an idyllic, close-knit community based on the best we have known. Even somewhere without clear boundaries which has been engulfed by decades of city growth will always remain a village in the mind of someone who knew it in 'the good old days'. In this book I have therefore chosen to record the stories of elderly villagers from places which have been swamped by development as well as those more clearly associated with chocolate-box images such as rows of thatched cottages, roses round the door and the goose-girl driving her birds up the lane.

Throughout the British Isles, certain 'characters' have come to epitomise village life, from the friendly 'bobby' on his bike to the beaming vicar greeting parishioners at the church door. Here I describe the lives and 'adventures' of thirteen of these great country stalwarts. Aged between sixty-five and ninety-three, they recall the happiness and comradeship to be found in country communities throughout this century of unprecedented change. All have shown great loyalty to certain places, none more so than 83-year-old housemaid Margaret Jackson, who has spent her entire life in one village. However, their lives have not only been about smiling faces, mucking in together at haymaking and leaving doors unlocked. Here, too, is frank comment on the 'down side' of life, not least the poverty, primitive living conditions, ill-health, accidents and suicides suffered by most communities.

In the old days of relative isolation and slow transport most villages were necessarily very self-sufficient with, for example, their own butcher, policeman, vicar and doctor. Now, in the rush to achieve centralisation and economies of scale, many of these pillars of the small community have disappeared, often forcing folk to travel long distances for essential goods and services. Many of us would argue that this is not advancement.

Gone, too, are many of the buildings and institutions on which village life once thrived, especially churches, schools, shops and post offices. Now even village pubs are disappearing by the thousand as big-business breweries deem their charges uneconomic. Of course, some caring communities have railed and rallied to save their places of worship or learning, a few even raising sufficient funds to buy and run their precious store or inn: but overall the story has been one of protracted village decline.

Village life has been further impoverished by 'emigration' to towns, as so many jobs on the land have been lost; moreover better education generally has provided greater aspirations and opportunities further afield, and the 'natives' cannot afford housing in competition with richer incomers. Yet in many cases village populations have soared, not only through people living longer but also because of the 'immigration' of folk fleeing the stress of modern urban life. Many commute daily or weekly, while others turn

The village postman always brought local news and gossip as well as letters. This picture was taken at Godshill, Isle of Wight, in 1937 (courtesy of the Post Office)

Schoolchildren saluting the flag at High Bickington, Devon, on Empire Day, 24 May 1923

centuries-old cottages into mere holiday homes, in extreme cases producing what have become known as 'dormitory villages'. But in their defence, many of the 'incomers' have brought new ideas and much-needed vitality to places which had become very introvert and were in decay. Indeed, in their search for 'belonging', many 'foreigners' have brought welcome leadership and it is often they who have done most to maintain the fabric of village life, especially through organisations such as the parish council, historical societies and the Women's Institute. They are an essential bridge between the old and the new, bringing new life to villages which should ring to the laughter of local children rather than the cash-till of tourists.

There is no doubt that much of the great sense of community in old village life was due to traditional squirearchical society, which it has become fashionable to condemn. Yet there is no doubting the great loyalty and sense of belonging generated by the paternalism of yesteryear. Of course it was in his lordship's interest to look after his staff, but much extra was given through sheer kindness: even today some old villagers still receive handouts such as 'the parish coal'.

To me, living in a small country community is a compromise between the attractions of both wilderness and town life. How pleasant it is to be close to nature; but after a while I tire of talking only to the birds and the wind. Similarly, I love the theatre and good restaurants; but after only a weekend in the city I want to break free. What the village offers is relative closeness to nature plus the comradeship of kindred spirits.

My village has long lost its shop, post office and school, and it is halved by a road which becomes more dangerous by the day. But it boasts a thriving village hall, one of the best village fêtes in the country and a wonderful, centuries-old pub where 'old money' mixes freely with new and cricket is played regularly on the green opposite. When I go for a pint I can be sure that I will know most of the customers, and we all care for where we live. On paper, the pub belongs to a brewery, whose various managers and tenants have enjoyed mixed success. In reality, the pub belongs to the local people, as it is the hub of village life, irrespective of ownership and occasional changes of image.

That said, this place is much the same as elsewhere in that few real characters remain. Our vastly changed way of village and country life simply does not generate the colourful individuals of old, men and women whose faces are cracked with adversity and refusal to conform, but whose eyes sparkle with fun and friendship. Yet scattered throughout these islands, now often in sad isolation whether in town or country, many stalwarts remain. Here is my selection, to tell you how village life used to be and to reveal what they thought about each other.

BRIAN P. MARTIN
Brook, Surrey 1997

IN GOOD SERVICE

Margaret Jackson
Housemaid of Buckinghamshire

In pre-war days of relatively cheap labour virtually every 'big house' in every village had a generous complement of staff. Among the most indispensable were the innumerable housemaids, girls from mostly humble backgrounds who generally expected very little out of life and who knew their place in the 'pecking order'. Some were cruelly maligned as 'mere skivvies', yet the stalwart domestics of those days generally had considerably more social standing than their modern counterparts. Their pay may have been abysmal, but in a good house they were virtually part of their employer's family and inevitably displayed great loyalty and took much pride in their work. Other, newer forms of employment may have tempted with higher wages, but they could not offer dignity, as Miss Margaret Jackson recalls: 'There were new factories in our area, but on no account would Mother let me go to them as that was considered degrading. Mother had always been in good service herself; you could tell that by the way she spoke and conducted herself.'

Thus it was no surprise that, at the age of sixteen, Margaret followed the family example. Her three older sisters were already in service and her younger sister would soon follow suit, but Margaret was luckier than most in securing a local position. With her sisters working and living away (they only returned for holidays), pressure on the family purse and space at home had already been reduced, but Margaret was still required to live with her employer. Remarkably, she was destined to remain in her native village until the present day.

Edith Margaret Jackson was one of seven children, and always known to her dearest as Meg. She was born on 13 July 1913 at the Buckinghamshire village of Wavendon, 'within the sound of the anvil' as her cousin was a blacksmith there. Sadly she never really knew her father, a timber worker and general labourer who helped build houses in the village: he suffered consumption (tuberculosis) for years and died when Margaret was only three. Fortunately, Margaret had a 'wonderful' mother to care for her, and she remembers her early years with great nostalgia.

'People helped each other much more then, and we were well supported by the love of our neighbours when Father died. Also, they made up for much of what we missed out on financially, people often bringing us things such as fruit and eggs.

'My earliest recollection is of a very simple gesture: picking a strawberry and showing it to Mother. The garden had everything in it in those days: a really lovely Blenheim, a greengage tree, plums, lots of gooseberries, and that lovely maiden's blush round the door – roses don't smell like that now.'

Margaret's grandfather also died young, in his forties. He once kept the village post office, but was better known as PC Collyer, the last resident policeman for Wavendon. However, he had not looked forward to being posted there because the place was notorious for 'the rough element'. The area was once known as Hogsty End, combining most of Woburn Sands with Wavendon.

Wavendon Oddfellows group (including Margaret's father) in the late nineteenth century

Happy in her work – a maid in service in the 1920s

Wavendon is unusual in having had only three clergymen in over 150 years, and the strength of the church there had a great influence on Margaret from an early age.

'For a start we were blessed with a Church of England school. Every year we had an exam for the Bishop's prize, and once I was runner-up. The dear old rector always used to go up to London and choose the prizes himself. I suppose you could say I was clever at school, and I was certainly very happy there. The only lesson most of us hated was learning to sing with the modulator. We always started school with assembly, with a hymn and prayer, and the last lesson of the day was from the scriptures. That school served the village well then, with about seventy pupils within walking distance; now, however, it would have closed long ago if it weren't for people dropping children off in cars. It's all very different from when every pony and trap used to come along with candles in their lamps, and those of us on foot often had to go across the fields by full moon or lantern light.'

Some seventy years later, Margaret still treasures a few of her school books, not least her prize volumes and one containing her painstakingly prepared sewing patterns. She also cherishes thoughts of 'the many poems we used to learn by heart, all about Mary Queen of Scots and brave Horatius. The standard was very high.' But of course not everyone was academically inclined, including Margaret's brother Hugh.

'Opposite the school was the slaughterhouse where the pigs were taken, and if "it" happened in the afternoon all the boys would go out to watch. They used to stand on the forms at the back of the class with their eyes out the windows. One day the teacher said to Hugh: "What's more interesting out there?" "Harry Gurney comin' up the road with a load of muck, sir," he replied. Hugh was only ever interested in farming and couldn't leave school quick enough. He and the other boys used to make the ink every week, using a powder, and us girls often got splattered.

'Mind you, the teachers weren't all perfect then. If our schoolmaster knew the Whaddon Chase hunt was meeting anywhere near he'd get off after them on his ol' bike, a lady's model. So the boys thought they'd go too. But Mr Buxton always knew who was missing and was heavy with the cane. Then one day he went berserk and the boys had him on the floor. Everybody was wringing their hands and didn't know what to do – but next morning nothing at all was said.'

The Jacksons lived in a simple cottage, one of fifty-three homes which have disappeared from the parish since Margaret was a girl. They encountered considerable hardship, although Margaret also remembers the many happy days during her childhood, just after the Great War.

'In 1921 the village purchased a disused Canadian army hut, and as the first scout group had just been formed it became known as the BP (Baden Powell) Hut. The day it opened was a red letter day for us. I can see it now, and all the fun times we had in it. Mothers, fathers and children were all so delighted to join in the festivities, playing musical chairs and tripping up the long room with Charlie the postman on the piano and all singing "A hunting we will go . . .". The scout group had a band in which my brothers Fred and Hugh played the kettle drums. When they marched through the village with flags flying we sisters ran alongside trying to keep up. Now that hut and the school have gone.

'As we paid under £5 a year rent we received "the parish coal": one ton a year dumped at your gate free of charge, courtesy of the Duke of Bedford's estate. We had lovely great lumps then and the boys barrowed it into the barn. And if you had more than a dust-panful of dust to sweep up after, you'd complain! Today there aren't the number of people applying for free coal, and if you get two hundredweight you're lucky.

A typical scout group band outside the local saddler

'When the milkman came, by pony and trap from a local farm, he often had a rabbit for a shilling, and that would do us two meals done in a brown earthenware jar in the oven. Then Tommy Allen, the rag-and-bone man who came round with a donkey, would give us sixpence for the rabbit skin, so the rabbit really cost us only sixpence.

'On Sundays Mum stayed home to cook while us children went to Sunday school and church. When we came home we had lovely beefsteak pudding and vegetables, and this would fill us up so we didn't want so much roast beef afterwards, making it a cheaper meal. That was the general trend for all the working people then, and it was the only time of the week a family would sit down together. There was no electricity, and everything was cooked on a coal-fire range. We never had a sweet after Sunday lunch, but Mother would have made a pie or tart on the Saturday and we'd have that with cold vegetables and other things after church on Sunday evening.

'Mr Neale, the baker, used to go round the houses, and on a Saturday he'd bake your cake for you. We used to love going in the bakery to hear the crickets.

'In the week there was always jam roll or spotted dick on the menu. And in the winter when we came home from school we would open the door and smell dripping toast for tea – that was a lovely thing to greet hungry children. And darling Mum was always there to welcome us.

'We lived very close to the school and always envied the "dinner" kids – those who lived more than one and a half miles from school. They always brought the first spring flowers, the crab blossom, and if snow was coming or a thunderstorm was threatening they'd be sent home early.

'No matter how poor we were we never wore on Sunday what we wore on Saturday. We always had pretty little cotton dresses and pinafores, a lot made at home by my sisters, and nice little warm coats in winter. We had long plaits, but our hair was loose on Sundays, with a bow.

'During 1920 terrible diptheria swept through the village; we all had it and the school was closed. Afterwards the whole school was disinfected, and that smell was in every pen, pencil and book for years. Darling Mother nursed we, her three young children, alone for fifteen weeks; and then, on a lovely day in February, a dear young cousin called Rosy brought the first snowdrops. She put them on a broom and lifted them up and I opened the bedroom window and took them in. It was so wonderful to smell those flowers and the fresh air after being indoors for so long. I can smell them now.

'One of my hobbies was recording the weather and I used to measure the winter solstice with the almshouse roof, in the yard nearby. We had some real winters then! We always had a slide in the road, and one lady used to come out to peel her potatoes on the ice to make it melt. We also had our whipping tops – known as "window breakers" – and hoops, and we used to go all the way to Walton. The "snob" (Collins the cobbler) used to put the peg in the top for us, and when we sang "Uncle Tom Cobley and All" we used to end up with "Snob and all".

'In the autumn we used to go acorning for Mr Gurney's pigs, and if there was a gale the children always went "sticking" for fuel. In those days I don't think anyone complained when children were missing from classes because the schools were so crowded. I still can't pass a bit of rotten wood.'

Despite the hardships, there were several annual treats to look forward to. For the Jacksons, the highlight of the summer holiday was a trip to Bedford, 'a lovely little town then', where two of Margaret's sisters were in service. 'We'd go into Woolworth's there and nothing was above sixpence. I still use the little birthday book I bought then.'

But for some thirty children of all ages the highlight of the whole year was the choir treat and Margaret remembers it well.

'Margate was the favourite destination. The train left Woburn Sands station at 5.30 am, so we always used to wake everybody up with all the noise we made, and we would reach the coast at about 9.30. The first thing we did was hire a deckchair, and I always ended up sunburnt. Then there was a lovely lunch and a fish-and-chip tea, and we always bought presents for those left at home. We generally returned about midnight.

19

Dear old Reverend Phillpotts paid for it all – he even gave us our spending money. That went on right up to 1939.

'The choir always went round carol singing on Christmas Eve: first we went up to the Rectory, then Tower House, and ended up at Wavendon House about 10pm, where there'd be a lovely supper laid on for us.

'The bellringers always started getting ready for Christmas on 5 November. At first they practised only once a week, but it ended up being daily. Nowadays they're not allowed to ring on Christmas Eve for fear of disturbing people, but us children used to love lying in bed listening to them: it was part of Christmas.

'We never had much in the way of Christmas presents. At first we just had a sugar mouse, an apple and orange, and perhaps a few pennies, all in the toe of a stocking. But later there might be a book by Angela Brazil or a jack-in-the-box, and if we were very lucky a flaxen-haired doll peeped out the top.

'But getting ready for Christmas was half the fun, with all that fruit to be washed and puddings and cakes to be made. There were three shops in Wavendon then and one was run by a dear old spinster, Miss Stradling. People used to say: "Have you seen her window? She's decked it out for Christmas." And what a lovely job she made of it. In the middle was an old oil lamp and we children used to gaze in at all the wonders carefully placed around it, looking at what we hoped to get for Christmas: dolls, toy pianos,

Carol singing has long been a popular village activity

*Musical chairs at Wavendon Church Sunday School New Year party,
with the Reverend C. L. Elliot on the fiddle*

skipping ropes, tops, dulcimers and nets of sweets. And when Miss Stradling put the light out in the darkness of the evening it was a sign for us all to go home. We used to buy our wooden hoops there, too. There was everything in that shop – even a chair to sit down on if you were tired.

'Then there was Percer's shop, where they had a great many ramshackle old bikes – you could hire one for a halfpenny for half-an-hour to learn to ride. If we were lucky we had a penny pocket money on a Saturday, and what you could buy for a penny then was nobody's business!

'The other big treat was the Sunday school party, usually on about 1 January in the school. We only had plain bread and butter, plain rice cake and fruit cake, but it was lovely because we sat down with the lady from Wavendon House, with her fine china and silver teapot. Wavendon House was the squire's house and Mrs Bond who lived there was like the Queen Mother to us.

'After the meal the seats were rearranged, out came the harmonium and we sang carols while we waited for the parents to come for the marionettes show; everybody was invited and it used to be packed out. If we had anything in the village today hardly anybody would turn up, but in the old days everybody went to everything.

'When the puppets were over we had the presentation and prizes for the marks we had gained in Sunday school. And we always finished with the national anthem, and three cheers for the rector. And when we went outside all the children were given an orange and a bun. We'd sing the national anthem on any occasion then, and on Empire Day we'd salute the flag, too.'

Empire Day dancers at Wavendon endowed school, 24 May 1923.
Margaret is in the middle row, sixth from the left

Like so many clever children of her generation, Margaret was denied the opportunity to go on to higher education because her family just could not afford to keep her. As a result, she left school at the customary age of fourteen 'in floods of tears'. But there was no full-time job for her to go to at first, and she was sixteen before she went to work as a housemaid for widow Waudby at The Old Rectory. Margaret describes those early days in service:

'I was a general help to everybody, but especially the cook and senior maid. There was also a chauffeur, a gardener and a garden boy. Mrs Waudby was a marvellous artist who had exhibited at the Royal Academy, and she had over seventy paintings in the drawing room alone. There were others all over the house and they took us ages to dust!

'My wages were about 10s a week, and I slept right at the top of the house. In 1939–40 it was so cold the water tanks were frozen solid, and at night, Edith the maid and I would be covered in ice where we'd breathed. So we had to go down and sleep in the guest chambers. In 1940 three lovely young men from the RAF were billeted with us, but they didn't mind the cold so much.

'The main reason why housework was much harder then was that there was no electricity, and no such thing as vacuum cleaners; it was all lamps and candles, dustpans and brushes. But we still managed to have fun.

'Edith always called Mrs Waudby at 7.30am and took her hot milk. She also took up hot water for washing, in lovely brass cans which we had to clean every day along with the silver candlesticks. Mrs Waudby took breakfast in her room at 9am and she'd be down by 10am, going straight into the Oak Room in winter. Her great creed was: "You never got a cold through being cold", and as a result there were only ever four fires lit

22

in that great house, including the kitchen range. But at least the house was lovely and cool in summer.

'Poor old Mr Paxton the coachman/chauffeur (a descendant of Sir Joseph Paxton) used to be perished when he got down off the carriage – but Mrs Waudby was always nice and warm inside with a lovely sable rug. Even so, he hated it when he was given a car. There was also a brougham and a two-seated, two-wheeled dog cart. Mr Paxton had special livery for summer and winter as well as Sunday. The brougham was very handy in the war for one of the young RAF men billeted with us: he had a tendency to stay out late with the girls, but Mr Paxton had told him that the house doors would be locked at a certain time, and that was that. So if he was too late to get in, the young man used to sleep in the brougham and come creeping in when he saw Mr Paxton light the fires first thing in the morning.

'As well as general cleaning I made the beds and did mending and sewing. And when the fruit came in ripe I had these great big trugs of gooseberries and other berries to top and tail. But for much of the time it was quite easy work, really, and we didn't reckon to be working all the time; for example I was generally up about 7am but there wasn't much to do in the afternoon when the lady went calling. We had much more work when visitors came, however, and I'd have to look after Mrs Waudby if Edith and Mrs Paxton were out for the day. In the morning I wore a blue check cotton dress and in the afternoon I was smarter, with a black dress and white apron to receive people. We always knew when Mrs Waudby was coming back because one of her dogs – a Kerry Blue terrier – always barked when her carriage was on its way.

'There was this wonderfully scented magnolia tree, and Mrs Waudby would cut one of its flowers and put it in a wicker basket to take to a friend when visiting. I think the tree must have been there since the house was built, in about 1850; but sadly it died in the frost of 1940.

'One of the worst upheavals was spring-cleaning, especially with all those pictures and clutter about, and after the sweep had been in to clear the birds' nests from the bed-room chimneys. It used to take two of us a whole week just to spring-clean the drawing room – we needed a day just to empty it. The carpet had to be taken out onto the lawn where the garden boy beat it; but he couldn't help bringing bits of lawn back in with it. When we did the spring-cleaning Mrs Waudby would go away with Mrs Paxton to a hotel for a week or so.

'The curtains were taken down and changed and cleaned several times a year. In spring and summer they'd be white lace tied with green bows, and the gardener would bring in white arum lilies; when autumn came they were changed to a thick, dark red material and the gardener brought in those lovely chrysanths.

'Mrs Waudby would never take a chair near the fire, and would often sit alone with just one lamplight in that enormous sitting room. Even in the dining room there was just one silver oil lamp in the middle of this huge table, and I often heard the gentle-men cursing because they couldn't see to carve the game or joint.

'We kept some things in the cellar because that was the coolest place in the house, but sometimes it flooded and had to be pumped out. One day I went down to fetch the cream jug and there was a great big toad in it; I had to tell Mrs Waudby, but she just smiled.

'Mrs Waudby never, ever went to the kitchen; I suppose she just trusted us. The only exception was at Christmas when she came in to see the wonderful staff decorations, as she had none of her own. You should have seen the holly among the gleaming copper pans!

'Mrs Waudby's old wireless had ear-phones, and all the wires ran under the carpet. There were three sets of earphones and whoever was there of a Sunday was allowed to listen to the service as long as they didn't make a noise; though it was difficult not to when taking the earphones out of the box.'

When the war started, Margaret joined the ARP first aid and went to lectures at Woburn Sands. Mr Paxton joined the Home Guard, which Margaret regarded as 'the biggest joke of all: he always said he was glad he joined because the only way he kept warm was through wearing their overcoat. When the water tanks froze we had to let the kitchen range go out and it was perishing.'

It was during the war that Margaret

took her 'nicest holidays ever', when her brother-in-law Bill was stationed at Banff, on the Scottish coast. She went there three times on the 'puffing Billy' (steam train), 'which changed its tune when it got to the top of the hill and went down again. It took twenty-four hours to get there and you couldn't move in the carriages for khaki.' That was quite an adventure for Margaret, because before that her annual fortnight's holiday was usually spent not far away, visiting an aunt at sedate Leamington Spa.

Things were 'a bit on the tough side' during the war, when 'thousands of Wrens were stationed in the area', as Margaret recalls:

'We had to eke out most things because of the rationing, but we got by. Most people took on allotments and many shared out their produce. But clothing was very difficult, and you could easily get rid of your allowance in no time at all.

'One of my worst memories is seeing that terrible red glow in the sky when they blitzed London in 1941. And there was that awful night they bombed Coventry, when the houses shook with all the bombers going over. One old lady I knew said: "They've been going over all night. They've shook the firmament and I haven't got a dry thread left in my body." But at least we didn't get any bomb damage at Wavendon.'

After some twelve years at The Old Rectory, Margaret spent about a year working at another local house, where her wages increased three-fold and the hours were only 8am

Happy in domestic service – Margaret (left) and friend

to 3pm; she found it 'a piece of cake', particularly as it was equipped with more up-to-date appliances. But then she had to go to help with the war effort, and work at a factory on the outskirts of the village, making transistors for the Navy. However, she had liked the new house so much that she still called in there each day on the way to the factory.

When the war ended Margaret went to The Tower to work as housemaid for the Marler family. 'They were very agreeable people, estate agents, and I was happy there for eleven years, until the family moved away. The only hard work I had to do was endlessly washing pairs of breeches because Major Marler and his elder son used to go out hunting with the North Bucks Beagles so much, often two or three times a week.'

Like so many others, Margaret regarded the ending of the war as a major turning point in the British way of life.

'Once it was over, everything we held dear disappeared: the women didn't want to stay at home any more, and that was the beginning of the home life breaking up; and the large staffs went from the big houses.'

Gone were the days when people were content to 'get round the lamplight in winter to play ludo or snakes and ladders': a new spirit of independence was prevalent. People generally became financially better off, they were more mobile, and they wanted to venture further afield; and with so many folk looking at life beyond their native haunts it was not surprising that village life and community spirit gradually deteriorated. Margaret's home patch suffered more than most because it was engulfed by 'new town' development: her observations are tinged with considerable sadness:

'When the Marlers moved away, that lovely house, The Tower, went to Milton Keynes Corporation for their headquarters, and there they planned the destruction of thirteen of our beautiful villages, including Milton Keynes itself. It's criminal that the new town should have taken the name of that delightful little place – there'd been a wonderful Bible with a chain through it in the village since Cromwell's day. The town should have had a new name. Later The Tower went to an American firm. You have no idea the lovely buildings that have gone, that used to be round that old house.

'In Wavendon there used to be four pubs: The Red House, The Plough, The Wheatsheaf and also The Leathern Bottle, just over the road where the Ancient Order of Oddfellows used to have a Whit Monday feast in the room attached. The carthorses used to be shod at The Red House, and it was wonderful watching the children help blow the bellows and seeing the sparks fly. We used to love singing that song: "Busy blacksmith, what are you doing at your smithy all day long . . ." I expect you know it – Handel wrote the tune. Now two of them are private houses. All the old chaps used to have their own special places and seats in the pubs. There was much more drunkenness then – it was quite usual to see men staggering about the village, but people used to respect the policeman, and there was never much trouble.

*Margaret (right) with the landlady of The Leathern Bottle and the old local lodge banner
which had lain unnoticed in a pub storeroom for thirty years*

'But there are not the characters around now, people like Charlie the postman, who wouldn't finish till gone three on Christmas afternoon and often called whether he had letters or not. He used to see you in the window and shout up things like "You've got a postcard, but you won't like it!" Nothing was sacred then.

'Another great character was the old verger, who held office for many years. She tolled the bell and tended the lamps, as there was no electricity in the church; if one started to burn low she'd stand on a pew, pull the lamp down and fill it. She often left an oily mess and smell on the pews, so you had to watch where you sat. Also, if anyone misbehaved in church she would tell them to leave. The rector called her "Boss". He never charged to marry people in church, but would say: "Give Boss half a crown".

'There used to be a great many vagrants, mostly begging for hot water for a cup of tea. One old couple used to come round regularly and Mum gave them slices of bread and dripping. How they survived just sleeping in the hedgerows I'll never know, especially as we used to have such cold winters. The worst I can remember was 1947, when the snow was ever so deep. You couldn't cross the fields, though the scenery was magnificent. I'd love to see another one like that: it would do everyone good.

'Tommy Dodd used to sweep the roads on a Saturday and everything was always tidy. Then there was one man from Northampton who used to open his van and there were all these shoes hanging up in rows – talk about a sight! The men used to buy all their heavy boots off him. And right up to the second war a tallyman came round from Stewkley on his bike and sold Mother articles such as tea towels. Another man went

27

round with a van and sold buckets and things. It was always easier to buy at the door when you didn't have a car or the time to spare.

'I never drove, but I wished I did. When I left The Tower I went back to the factory where I worked in the war, but things were very different then and you were in good company. It was convenient for me as Mother died in 1959 and I was on my own; also our cottage was deteriorating in condition so I went into a bungalow. Later I moved into this modern block, owned by Milton Keynes – and so I've come back onto my former stamping ground because this is where our house used to be. I still love the place and have some good friends – but life can be lonely in a flat, even with people so close; it's not so social. There's something very special about living in a cottage; on a nice day you can open the door and sit and watch the world go by. But you can't do that up all these steps. And you do miss the garden. In the old days you thought nothing of someone coming round with a bushel of peas.'

During the 1930s a great range of goods were sold door-to-door, either from horse-drawn carts, or by motorised transport

Although Margaret has many regrets regarding the demise of traditional village life, she has never been one to sit idly by and be overwhelmed by so-called progress. On the contrary, she remains very active in promoting community spirit. She even still rides a bike, 'but not too far', despite an accident about twenty-seven years ago in which she broke her hip. She has been closely involved with the church all her life, and after she retired from the factory, aged sixty, she was able to devote even more time to it.

'It's a full-time job, really. I was a member of the parochial church council for many years, and now I'm the verger, cleaner and sacristan, which means I look after the altar and sacred vessels. St Mary's Church dates back to the twelfth century, and we're very proud of the Grinling Gibbons pulpit, which is said to have been rescued from the Great Fire of London. We only have the one service now: Holy Communion on Sunday. It's just a matter of form, really – I don't like these new services – and then only thirty or forty people come. Anyone can take a service here now. In the old days we had 8am Communion, 11am Matins and 6pm Evensong.

'They never sing those lovely hymns now – the only chance you get to hear them is on TV. I was in the choir for thirty-five years, from 1925 until 1960, and I've nearly forgotten how to sing the Te Deum. I sung the solos when I was young, and we used to sing for funerals, too.

Mr R. Payne auctioning produce at the Wavendon Flower Show which was held in the Parish Hall and enthusiastically supported by young and old alike

'There was a time when you wouldn't get a seat at harvest festival evensong if you weren't there by 5pm. Now it's all different, but I've always stuck to the rule that Sunday should be separate. When we were young even shoes had to be cleaned on Saturday.

'We also used to have a great many lovely events outside the church; for example there was terrific fun with the village concerts and socials. What with "Wings Week" and "Soldiers' Week" to raise money for the troops, whist drives, parades and so on, there was something happening almost every night. And the children's nativity plays were beautiful, too. The British Legion was strong here once, but most of the people who ran it have become too old or have died.'

The British Legion marching through Wavendon; at one time it was strongly supported and contributed a great deal to the solidarity of a village (North Bucks Times)

However, not all has been doom and gloom in Wavendon since the war, and the spark of community hope long nurtured by Margaret Jackson has occasionally been coaxed into flame by celebrities who have adopted the village. John Betjeman came to read poems, famous actors and actresses visited, and The Old Rectory has become one of the homes of the internationally acclaimed musician and composer Johnny Dankworth and his celebrated jazz-singing wife, Cleo Laine. In the very house where Margaret once heard nothing livelier than the 'awful crackle' of those first wireless sets, the air became vibrant with innovation and creativity. The Dankworths turned the old stables into a theatre, and when this was extended Princess Margaret and the actress Joyce Grenfell were among the guests at the opening. For that very special occasion Margaret was invited to help out, and was delighted to wear her old maid's frock and apron again, 'just for a bit of fun'. But she did find it strange to wait at table in a dining room which she had known as a kitchen for so long, and she did have to laugh when Princess Margaret's detective asked if she was local!

Nowadays, when Miss Margaret Jackson talks to local schoolchildren about how village life used to be, she also enthuses about the occasion that Johnny wrote the mass and Cleo sang in church. She is proud to count the Dankworths as friends, and to be such an important link between very different generations.

A FAIR COP

FRANK PERCHARD
Policeman of East Sussex

In the old days the long-serving country policeman had plenty of opportunity to get to know villagers well, and this generally enabled him to apply the law more fairly and efficiently. Frank Perchard explains.

'I knew some policemen who'd been in their country stations for as long as twenty years, although this policy did change, the top brass coming to think that five years was enough in one job; they said that if the local policeman became too friendly with the locals it would lead to corruption. But in nearly all cases it didn't. In the country, on your own, *you* were the chief constable; but if you were fair to people there was a great deal of loyalty in return, to the extent that outside help was resented. And there was such protocol in the old days – for example, detectives always rang the village bobby when they wanted to make enquiries on his patch, to ask if that would be all right.

'Conmen never had much success in the country because every country copper knew his patch and the people in it so well, and anything out of order was soon noticed or reported. And you were well respected. People would never call me by my Christian name in the presence of the visiting sergeant or inspector; they'd always say "Good morning, Mr Perchard". And when I played village cricket the boys were always told by their parents to call me Mr Perchard on the field until they went out

As a young man Frank served in the Palestine police

to work. "Catch it, Mr Perchard!" you'd hear them shout. Otherwise it was Christian-name terms with the villagers – except with "the Squire". The true squire, Lord Brassey, had gone, but F. J. Parsons considered himself to be the new holder of the title and *he* would never call me by my Christian name.

'If you grew up with families it made all the difference, and local kids caught misbehavin' always reacted to what you said to them. It was important that you could name them all and not just address them as "you lot". When they said "But we're doin' nothing", I would say: "Well, go on home and do nothing there"; otherwise I knew that sooner or later they *would* do something.'

Frank's fairness was often rewarded, however, and a good example of this occurred one day when he was required to be on hand to sort out the traffic at a church wedding. He recalls the event with justifiable pride.

'I really wanted to be at a local cricket match, but I couldn't get the special constable to help, as I usually did. Officially I was on duty till 6pm, but when the wedding was over I was persuaded to umpire the match for the last hour. So after tea I cycled up and left my bike by the pavilion, as usual in a prominent position with my cape over the handlebars so that anybody could see where I was if I was needed.

'After a while the batsman said to me: "Hey Frank, there's two kids pinching your bike!" – but then I saw the area police car come in, and the sergeant got out to watch the game for a while, not realising that there was a policeman's uniform under that white coat! He had no idea I was there because those villagers had demonstrated their great loyalty by quickly telling the kids to wheel my bike out of sight. And I didn't feel guilty about going off duty a bit early because I always gave far more than needed. You were never really off duty.'

That incident was at Catsfield, in East Sussex, where Frank was the village policeman from 1957 until 1976, the most enjoyable period in a career for which he was well suited.

Francis William Charles Perchard was one of five children, and was born in the Sussex coastal town of Hove on 30 July 1927. He won a scholarship to Hove Grammar School (now a comprehensive), but left at sixteen to work for Clifford Edwards, the local marine engineers who made guns and aircraft fuel tanks. As a young man he served in the Palestine police from late 1946 until 1948, when the force was disbanded on the state of Israel being established. He returned home to live with his parents, but wanted to continue in the colonial police. He was advised to do a couple of years in a UK police force first, and was accepted by the Sussex police; he joined on 21 June 1949. After three months training at Sandgate he was posted to Bexhill-on-Sea, where he earned about £6 a week and his lodging cost £2 a week including laundry.

But then Frank's long-term plans were thwarted when he met Jean, the landlady's niece; they married in 1950 and, as Frank recalls:

'That was the end of me! I couldn't imagine her wanting to go out to Nyasaland or some other far-flung part of the British Empire, nor could I subject wife and baby to that, especially as living and education prospects were not good in Africa. Anyway, I'd started to like my job in the Sussex police.

'Bexhill was a quiet, genteel place then. In daylight hours you patrolled in full view of the public, but at night you went by the shops where potential miscreants couldn't see you. I also occasionally did duty at Battle, where you learnt to expect anything. One lady on holiday in Northumberland rang up just to ask me to go round to check that she'd turned off the gas!'

In 1957 Frank was moved to Catsfield, and at the time he had mixed feelings.

'Theoretically you could say no, but they'd soon find somewhere else for you. In many respects being posted to the country then was a consolation prize for not being promoted; in those days you were still thinking in terms of fifteen years to make sergeant – pre-war, anyone who made the grade under that was considered a "flyer". Things really started to change after the war, when a lot of ex-Army officers were coming in who demanded quicker promotion; and it was quite right, too. I remember one man having to sign for a police bike, yet he'd been the sergeant-major in charge of the vehicle park for the D-Day landings!

When Frank (middle row, extreme right) trained, in 1949,
his force wore flat caps rather than helmets

'But it was good to be your own boss out in the sticks. The superintendent would always ring up beforehand to say when he was coming, so we could put anything away that shouldn't have been there. My predecessor was heavily into winemaking, but you really couldn't get rid of the smell of that! In those days there was a special wireless room because the police were still very concerned with civil defence; but when we thought it wasn't needed it was soon used for other, unauthorised purposes!'

Frank also looked after the neighbouring village of Crowhurst, giving him a total population of some 2,000 people to care for. At first his only transport was a bicycle, which he remembers well.

'It was a big, sit-up-and-beg Vindec with a twin crossbar. Believe me, if you were dismounting from it with one of those long mackintoshes and you got a button caught you went down with a horrible crash. And the superintendent always made sure you could ride a bike before handing it over, making you go up and down in front of him. Later on I was issued with a new bike with gears; in fact this was a mistake but I refused to relinquish it!

'I didn't get a van till about 1967, by which time my old station had closed and I policed Catsfield, Crowhurst and Hooe from Ninfield. At first I had a green Mini van, but it gave me terrible backache so they allowed me to swap it for a Morris 1000, which was much better. But a van wasn't the same for local policing. A bike is quiet and easy to conceal so you can surprise people, but with a van the kids see you leave the village in a cloud of smoke.'

For Frank, 'one of the beauties of living in the country was having no fixed duty schedule'. He recalls how it suited his lifestyle.

'We only had the odd night duty and you could fix your own day duty as long as certain core hours were included. My favourite was 9am to 1pm and 7 to 11pm – "sem to leven" – because this enabled me to play cricket in the afternoon. The split hours were also useful for taking the wife shopping and doing a bit of gardening. But the introduction of the eight-hour shift stopped all that.

'However, with the split-hour system you could still be called out at any time, and at night people mostly used to ring the local bobby rather than dial 999; there was the odd time I had to go to a serious road accident in a pair of old flannels and slippers. But generally I kept a special night kit handy, with wellingtons and a blue pullover and such, so that I looked at least a bit like a policeman in an emergency.'

In a popular retirement area, and with an ageing population (many young folk having left the land to work in towns) exposed to greatly increased traffic, more and more of Frank's time was spent dealing with road accidents and sudden deaths. Furthermore, there had to be an inquest when the deceased had not been seen by a doctor for twenty-eight days. Frank recalls many incidents with great sadness.

'You can't help getting closely involved when someone you know dies. Once when a local shopkeeper died suddenly I didn't have to ask his widow a single question as I knew

The local bobby, pounding the beat in the mid-1950s. Not for him the steel cocoon of the patrol car, but a chance to get to know the people on his patch really well. Good relations with the locals often paid dividends: they trusted him and as a result were willing to give him snippets of useful information

them so well. But you can't go taking on everybody's grief as it happens so often. There's very few places I can pass between Battle and Bexhill without being reminded of a road accident or sudden death.

'I always carried a large pocket knife on my belt – not in the pocket, as that would soon be worn out – and over the years I had to cut down six suicides with that. My son, who is also a policeman, has that knife now.

'People also often kill themselves with gas ovens, but at least that's clean and tidy – other forms of suicide are much messier. It's mostly shotguns used in the country. One man put a screwdriver in a vice in his shed, looped the trigger-guard over it and jerked the gun back to shoot himself in the heart. Then there's those who lie on the railway line, an extremely messy method. But one man who cut his throat was very considerate when he did it over a bucket to catch the blood and even dropped the knife in. The sad thing is that people's reasons for killing themselves, such as money owed, are often of little or no consequence and generally could easily be put right. Sadly, the high incidence of suicides among farmers has continued in recent years, as many have suffered great financial pressure.

'I've known some terrible fatal accidents, too. In the country we were always told to ring for an ambulance first before going to any tractor we saw overturned in a field. With accessibility a problem in rural areas it was much better to make sure the experts were underway before charging across the fields to administer limited first aid. Nowadays there are far fewer farming accidents, with all tractors having roll bars fitted and much tighter control by the health and safety executive. Also, casualties generally receive help much more quickly now with better communications, better roads, better transport and air ambulances on hand for the worst incidents.

'Once at Ninfield an open-top tractor turned over on the road and squashed the driver flat. Another time a chap backed his tractor over his own child. The force has lost so many coppers who just can't get used to the sudden death of a child, and I never did. It's talking to the relatives that's hardest, but at least as friend and local policeman you can help to ease their pain by sorting out such matters as the undertaker.

'With so many folk engaged in hard physical work country people often suffer awful injuries, too, and sometimes it is really difficult to persuade them to seek medical help. This probably stems from ingrained suspicion of new ways and traditional independence and self-sufficiency among rural communities. Of course, as the local bobby you are often the first person people turn to for help and advice.'

Despite such tragedies, Frank often had reason to laugh with or at many of his fellow countryfolk, some of whom were quite eccentric. Here he relates some of his more entertaining experiences.

'Because village people know each other so well they can laugh and joke at each other's expense, and know just how far they can go before they offend. For example, my number was 257, so they often called me two tins of Heinz, that company being well known for its 57 varieties of canned food. And when I first took out the ol' bike at Catsfield a smart, middle-aged woman stopped me and asked if I was the new policeman. "Yes," I replied. "Oh," she said, "we were expecting an older man." I was then only thirty and, being quite young-looking, I was easily taken for a cadet. So I reassured her by saying: "May I quote, I think from Oscar Wilde, madam, that time will take care of that." "Oh," she said, "we have a literary policeman in the village: how delightful!"

'Another lady found my sunglasses when I left them at the cricket pavilion, and she took them home for safekeeping. When I went into the stores, in uniform, to buy a stamp, she happened to see me, and in front of everyone called out: "Frank, I've got your sunglasses in my bedroom!" The local people have never allowed me to forget that!

'Another outspoken person was the Irish JP up at the manor; he was always telling his gardener how his Italian servants were much more trustworthy than the British, but eventually this annoyed the gardener so much that he determined to get his own back, especially as he knew that the foreign servants in the manor only worked when the boss was there. So he grew some flowers in the shape and colour of the Union Jack, in a prominent position at the front of the house!

'Then there was the hot day when I was in my garden in scruffy old clothes and a lady came up the path. As she approached, she warned me away, saying: "I don't want you, I want the policeman!" So I just let her carry on and she put a note through my door. It said: "Please look after my house while I'm away." I thought to myself, the sooner you get to know me, the better madam!

'Yes, we had plenty of eccentrics in Catsfield, including a retired admiral who took part in the pub's runner-bean competition. He sewed two beans together and probably

In those days Hunts really were part of the fabric of village life, with a great following among farmers.
They were also important in providing work for farriers, saddlers, vets and tailors, as well as being the focus
of much social activity for the whole community

would have taken first prize because you couldn't see the join at all when they were all hanging up along the bar! But then he owned up.

'On another occasion the admiral wanted to wind up the licensee of The White Hart. He was a very clever man and wrote to the landlord in Russian, saying that a trade delegation was coming over and that certain food and rooms would be required. He even got me to supply a Russian stamp from my collection and he extended the frank marks on it onto the envelope. Then he got the postman to deliver the letter and the landlord really fell for it: he knew the admiral could speak Russian and asked him for a translation! But in the end the landlord was obviously going to such great trouble and expense that we had to own up!'

The White Hart was always very much involved in village activities, but it was never responsible for much disturbance, as Frank relates.

'There used to be many sizeable gatherings at the pub, including a meet of the East Sussex Foxhounds because the Master, Lord Burleigh, lived in the village. Personally I never saw much point in dressing up to cull animals, but I got on well with the Hunt, and when they met at The White Hart it made a lovely sight for my children.

'The police house was right opposite the pub, and I was used as a spur to get people

The village cricket team: a chance for the men of the village to exhibit their sporting prowess and an excuse for a bit of friendly (and sometimes not so friendly!) rivalry between neighbouring villages

out on time. The landlord used to say: "Come on ladies and gentlemen, the constable's got his office light on!"

'There was one incident at the pub which really sticks out in my mind. The White Hart was always the unofficial HQ of our Catsfield Cricket Club, and one day we were holding a fund-raising walk with fancy dress. When I went into the pub, I was immediately hemmed in by a crowd of club members so that I couldn't see what was going on: it turned out that someone was doing a sponsored streak up the road and across the pub car park, and the members didn't want to embarrass the local policeman in case it was illegal!'

Cricket has long been a mainstay of village life, an activity which truly binds the community together, generating loyalty and comradeship. Quite apart from providing a sporting arena where much pride is at stake for the players, it draws in entire families, with sons in the colts and wives providing the teas. Furthermore, it is increasingly a way in which 'outsiders' can become involved in village life.

The Catsfield Cricket Club was formed in 1799 and Frank played for it for twenty-five years, until 1983. He has also been chairman since 1984 and team secretary since 1975. He has survived this period with mixed emotions.

'They won't let you go, you know, even though I no longer live in the village. But

Churchwardens, stalwarts of the community, were drawn from all walks of life.
Their duties, which were many and various, were undertaken with a sense of great responsibility

now some of the youngsters must come forward and help with the admin. I still bash away at the team lists on my Olympic typewriter, which cost £30 new in 1957, when I had 10s 6d a quarter typewriter allowance from the police.

'We never fight over cricket here; we regard it purely as a recreation, and play only friendlies. The team is all local people and now includes two policemen from Battle – we can't have the actual Catsfield bobby as she's a woman!

'Fred Parsons, the JP and self-appointed squire, was president of the cricket club, but he also had his own estate team and my predecessor at the police station suggested that I should play for it twice a year, against Catsfield! "Do yourself a favour," he said, "I played for him, and now I've been promoted." But I could never do that, as I was completely loyal to the village team! In fact Fred became increasingly annoyed because the Parsons eleven kept losing against us, and he imported some ex-county players from all over.

'I was also asked to play cricket for the Hunt, which really appealed to me as they had some lovely fixtures. But their matches were midweek, and I made the silly mistake of asking the inspector at Battle if this was all right. "Certainly not," he said. "You must not be seen to align yourself with one side or the other." Yet my sergeant always wore the Hunt badge prominently. It certainly taught me never to ask permission!

'We were required to be fair and impartial on every front. Once when I was on holiday, Battle Young Conservatives pinned a poster to my official exterior notice board, advertising one of their dances. But when the chief happened to come by and see it, he said I had to advertise anything to do with the Labour Party, too!'

As the village policeman, Frank was also closely involved with the church. But his duty to God was not always straightforward, and even landed him in trouble.

'A new village policeman was always advised to seek out the rector as sometimes the two roles could work well together in many ways. However, the first one I knew was the Earl of Lauderdale, who probably succeeded to the title while in the job and was eccentric to say the least. Then came Arthur Talbot, who was down to earth and maintained that it didn't matter what people wore to church as long as they were there.

'Catsfield church was thriving. It had a churchyard oak going back to the Domesday Book, though the top of the tree became dangerous and had to be taken down. Also dangerous was the position of the church, on a hump in the road with the churchyard opposite. This meant that as the amount of traffic increased I often had to be on hand at funerals to see the coffin safely across the road. Once as I stood in the road I felt something cold on my leg, and this woman was actually nudging me with her car because she wanted to get by, even though I clearly had my hand up! In those days this sort of thing was laughed off, but anyone trying it now would be done for assault.

'I also had to control the traffic at church services. But after a while the rector said to me: "You don't want to be here every Sunday. Why don't you put out some cones?" So I did. Then one day he said: "Tell you what, leave the cones here in the porch and I'll put them out," which we did. But when HQ found out they were furious! "Those cones are not legal unless they are put out by a police officer," they said; and they were right.

'But we did have our lighter moments at church. One day I was standing with my bike by the church gate, talking to the Reverend Talbot, when this lady said to me: "Oh, please don't move! I want to take your photograph together. The Reverend looks after us in heaven and you look after us on earth." '

Another task of the village policeman was to help prevent and contain the spread of disease among animals. Frank describes some of his main duties in this field.

'The local policeman was the inspector under the Diseases of Animals Acts, and among the things I was required to do was to supervise sheep dipping, the burial in lime of any cattle with anthrax, and the burning of other stock. We took diseases very seriously then, which is why we have such good control today. But the system was less efficient in that some postings brought in policemen who knew nothing about country life and animals.

'When there was an outbreak of fowl pest all eggs, chicks and grown birds within a two-mile radius had to be destroyed. I never knew any farmers to object, but then they did get compensation. The only time I remember fowl pest causing an upset was when Fred Parsons' pheasants had to be destroyed. He lived for pheasant shooting and was nearly reduced to tears. When I first met Fred, at the flower show, he immediately asked me: "Do you shoot?" I said I didn't, but he saw my point of view and respected it.'

Occasionally Frank was called to help animals involved in accidents, and for one particular rescue he and a colleague each received a certificate of commendation from the RSPCA. He describes what happened:

'An 18-hand showjumper from a nearby stables had fallen into Pevensey Marshes and exhausted itself trying to scramble out. So Sergeant Bert Turner and I jumped in and managed to keep its head above water until the fire brigade arrived with their lifting tackle. We managed to keep the horse alive – but back at the station we were told by the guv'nor that we could safely have left the entire affair to the fire brigade, instead of messing about in water!'

There were other occasions, too, when Frank was reprimanded for giving a helping hand. He recalls a second incident involving the fire brigade.

'They were having trouble with their water supply, so my colleague and I whacked away with flails in the middle of a gorse fire at Cooden. When we returned to the police station, dehydrated and with faces like beetroots, we learnt that the fire chief had phoned to express his thanks. But his views were not endorsed by the guv'nor, who declared: "Your job is to find out who starts fires, *not* to mess about putting 'em out!" '

There has also been considerable difference of opinion in recent decades where an increasing number of people have moved from town to countryside, but have not understood or accepted traditional country ways. Frank recalls some of their misunderstanding and fears:

'Once a pig was reported "at large" in Bexhill high street, after it had escaped from a lorry. But when it was caught it starting squealin' away as the driver tried to get it on his vehicle, and this lady called out: "Officer, stop that man mistreating that pig!" But, of course, he wasn't – you only have to breathe on a pig to make it squeal. So I gave a hand in getting it loaded.

'Many townies move out to the country and then complain about the silliest things, such as cockerels crowing and cows and their calves lowing constantly for twenty-four hours or so after they've been separated at weaning. They plead with you to do something about it, though of course you can't, as much as you can't do anything about the foxhounds sounding like the hounds of the Baskervilles while they are waiting to be fed.

'I must admit that I was occasionally apprehensive or puzzled by some things, even the ordinary sounds of the country night, when I moved out from the town. When I first heard a cow cough behind a hedge I wondered what was going on, because it sounded exactly like a human cough. But then I thought, if it's someone up to mischief he wouldn't cough here and now, nor so loudly.'

Then there are the busybodies and others who jump to conclusions. Frank remembers one incident in particular when things were not what they seemed.

'I looked out from the police station and saw this little boy picking dandelion leaves along the grass verge, presumably just gathering greenstuff for his rabbit. However, I knew that the council had recently drenched the verge with a noxious weedkiller so I rushed out in my shirtsleeves to stop the boy poisoning his pet or even himself. I took the carrier bag from him, tipped the contents out and told him to wash his hands – in fact I took him into my kitchen to make sure he did so.

'However, a lady had been watching all this from her parked car, and wrote anonymously in a complaint to my sub-division about a nasty policeman frogmarching into the station a little boy who wasn't doing anything wrong. I was called before the inspector to explain, and when I did so, he of course simply binned the letter. But the story provides a good lesson for police recruits, who need to bear in mind that complaining people will invariably resort to monstrous embellishment.'

Over the years Frank has seen some significant changes in police uniform and equipment, but has certainly not been in favour of them all.

'I don't agree with chief constables appearing on TV in woolly pullovers: it's just too casual and gives a bad impression. In the old days we always had a closed-neck tunic and you could wear what you wanted under it in cold weather – though not too much, otherwise the buttons would strain a bit. So you had to go up a size. It was a great advantage for early turn, as you could be up and about in minutes. It took much longer to get ready when they brought in a tie, detachable shirt collar and studs; and you always had to be on duty ten minutes before your start time. It was fifteen minutes in some forces, though that doesn't happen now.

'When they brought in shirts with fixed collars they said we couldn't wear the old pale blue ones with detachable collars. Well, I had a stack of the old ones as good as new and I didn't want to waste them, so I took them all down to The White Hart and gave them away.

'We only wore caps at first. The East Sussex force had given up helmets in 1921 and they didn't come back in until 1953, with the coronation. Then a lot of people didn't know how to wear them properly, and there's nothing so silly as a policeman's helmet which is too big and on the back of his head: it must be well forward to be dignified.

'We used to have an allowance of about 2s 6d a week for ankle boots, and you couldn't have toecaps; but now police can wear shoes of just about any type as long as they're black.

'A whistle was compulsory then, but I never used it. In the city the idea was to summon assistance from the man on the next beat, but in the country who on earth would come? The only time my whistle was used was when a Catsfield football referee left his at home!

'I never used a truncheon, as it was too dangerous to carry. It's supposed to fit in a special long pocket inside your trousers and be tucked in by a flap so that the public can't see it and be frightened. When I first had one I was visiting this lady and happened to admire a book on her bottom shelf. But when she invited me to take a look and I bent down, the truncheon caught between my legs and nearly caused extreme damage! So I never wore it again, except on official parades. But it was good as a garden dibber for putting in cabbage plants.

'For our notebooks we always carried an indelible pencil or ink pen, as ordinary pencil could be rubbed out. We recorded our movements at the front of the book, and details of incidents at the back. Front entries had to be clear and precise, but we were always told that whatever you wrote at the back of your notebook should only mean something to you.

'You always left details of where you were going – say, outside Boots at 9 o'clock and the church at 10 o'clock – back at HQ; then if a sergeant or inspector wanted to see you, he knew exactly where to go. He'd come out, test you with questions on the law and other things, ask to see your notebook and then initial it. But once they trusted you to be at certain points at certain times they didn't bother checking up very often.

'Communication was always difficult before mobile phones. In the villages I had to phone in regularly to Battle to say where I was, and if they wanted me they often had to work out where I might be, phone the nearest public call-box and ask whoever answered if there was a policeman nearby!

'At my police house, built in 1921, there was a bell for the telephone at the bottom of the stairs; but my predecessor had stuffed a sock in it, and the bell at the bottom of the garden wasn't functioning either. In those days police houses always had a big garden to keep you busy and make sure you were there when wanted! Now there's two houses built in my old garden. As elsewhere, the sergeant had a key to my office, but not to the rest of our house.'

Frank considers himself lucky to have become a country copper during an era which was just beginning to disappear. On the whole there was relatively little serious crime to cope with, and the methods of dealing with most offences were significantly different. Here Frank describes how it used to be:

'During my first five years at Catsfield I never dealt with a single burglary in the village, and precious few outside. Sacrilege was almost unheard of then, whereas nowadays virtually all the churches in the area have been vandalised or broken into. And the only time I was ever attacked was in Battle, never in the villages. Mind you, in those days if you had a go at a policeman you were soon shown the way home; nowadays the police have to be so careful with complaints, so it's much more difficult to give a firm hand. Now, if someone says the handcuffs are too tight you must be extra careful – though in the past we knew that such an old chestnut generally meant the person would try to escape.

'The attitude of the bench used to be very different, too. The older magistrates always seemed just to *know* when someone was guilty, and they always gave us great support: one used to say to the defence counsel: "Stop badgering my policeman!" Once a vicar was in court and his defence stressed how much the oath meant to him. So this magistrate angrily said to the lawyer: "Are you trying to say that the oath means nothing to *my* policeman?"

'The great advantage of being a country copper was that you were dealing with agreeable, upright, decent people most of the time, who rarely challenged what I said. There was no need to inflate the evidence if it was there.

'It has changed for the worse with all these summary offences, too. In a small community it was often much better to deal with things by just a quiet word. With overdue car tax, for example, I'd say: "The old excise licence looks a bit whiskery John. Tell you what, you get one tomorrow and show me the day after." Nowadays the majority of traffic wardens are singularly offensive: they're just revenue gatherers, and are sent out on the streets with virtually no experience.

'I can't remember how many stories I've heard for no road fund licence. One woman said: "The baby's eaten it!"; and then there was the old lady who thought they lasted for ever. Another had been told to bring in her documents, and when she came I asked to see her MOT certificate' "What's that?" she said. So I explained, to which she replied: "Young man, I don't have time to clamber about under a car doing all that!"

'Another thing that's changed is that not so many people have pride in a place now.

Take the bus shelter outside the pub, for example; when I was at Catsfield it was like a new pin, but just look at it now. As soon as there's no bobby nearby, people start to abuse things. Nowadays most police don't live near their beats, and as soon as their duty's over they're off home. And those who do live on the spot are more interested in watching TV rather than getting out and helping to organise things such as youth activities. In those days us policemen used to take part in *all* village activities, from the drama club to tennis and flower shows; but then so did most of the other villagers, too. That bound people together and they took a real pride in where they lived.'

According to Frank, lost property and lost dogs have long been the bane of a policeman's existence.

'Sorting these out was supposed to have been taken over by local authorities years ago, but they've been dragging their heels over it. I always used to get the probationer to take lost dogs to the dogs' home at Bexhill, but one day he objected, complaining that he didn't look dignified while walking this poodle along the street; to which I replied: "I don't care if you carry it or put it in a bag, but you get it there!"

'We didn't have so much to do with the RSPCA over lost animals, only over a few cases of animal cruelty, mainly to dogs and pigs; usually this was just neglect, thoughtlessness really, where animals weren't cared for properly while owners were away. The difficult thing was proving it.

'We had considerable trouble with unexploded ammunition being found in the area. In the war there were a great many soldiers based here, and when they went to France on D-Day they hastily buried a large number of unwanted live grenades; even today these World War II relics still turn up, sometimes being brought to the surface by a farmer's ploughing. Some of the incidents we had to deal with were extraordinary. For example, workmen building an extension to a wartime ex-officer's house unearthed what he thought was a mortar bomb; it was indeed what he suspected – although instead of being tarnished and corroded, it was bright and shiny. "I thought you said it had just been dug out of the ground," I observed. "Oh yes, it was," he replied: "but I couldn't possibly hand it to you in its dirty state so I shone it up with turps and a wire brush!"

'Another instance of dicing with death involved a lady who kept a live grenade on her mantelpiece and used it for breaking coal! Then there was the small boy who found a live grenade in a field and slept with it under his pillow for a week, with the knowledge of his mother!'

Like many long-serving policemen, Frank met a few distinguished and well-known people during his service. He also soon learned not to judge anyone by their looks.

'One day I saw this "thing" approaching the station, with earrings, tattoos and a shaven head, and immediately I was suspicious. But all he wanted was to know where the hospital was so that he could deliver toys to the children. I felt that small!

'Then there was an old boy at Crowhurst who didn't look anything special, but I discovered he'd been Kitchener's driver in World War I and for a short time also Monty's driver in World War II; after which he was an instructor at Hendon police driving school.

'But Harry Corbett, the actor, who used to live near us, could never be taken for the wrong person: I always remember him saying to me: "I'm Steptoe. Olivier can be anybody, but I could only ever be Steptoe!"

'I suppose the most famous person I've ever seen was President Kennedy; he came over to see Macmillan and I was among the extra police called in for security. He had his own secret service bodyguards with him, and they wanted to eat with the British bobbies in the tent especially provided – but I bet they wished they hadn't when we were served those horrible rubbery eggs!

'The service was always trying to economise, just as it does today. It was always said that a superintendent's main function was to keep expenses down, so it was common, for example, to have old telephone directories as substitute toilet rolls. And whenever there was heavy snow the chief constable sent round a message saying that all country coppers had to stand by their stations. Perhaps he was more interested in preserving police vehicles than helping people!'

In 1963 Frank took a detective training course at Bexhill, but he didn't like the work; so when it was over he decided to return to his old patch as country copper. His old station has been closed down, however, and in addition to Catsfield he had to look after Ninfield, which became his new base. He retired as a country copper in 1976, but worked for a further five years in the enquiry office at Battle, a traditional late-service posting with less exacting duties. However, he would have been more than happy to have stayed at Catsfield for the rest of his life.

Frank now lives at Battle with his wife and one of their two daughters, in one of the old police houses which they were able to buy as sitting tenants when the terrace behind the station was sold off. He remains very active in retirement and retains strong links with the force, especially as his only son is the village policeman at Beckley, near Rye; he, too, will soon be coming up for a long-service award!

While Frank is happy at Battle, his heart remains in nearby Catsfield where he is still publicity officer for the horticultural society, a member of the village hall refurbishment committee, and poster producer for the dramatic society and other organisations. When I asked him what made it such a special village when he worked there, he replied: 'A general lack of pretentiousness prevailed there. It was a place where every man was not only equal, but seen to be equal. I've seen an ex-captain taking a bowl of soup to some old villager there, and when you see that sort of thing you know it's a good place to live.'

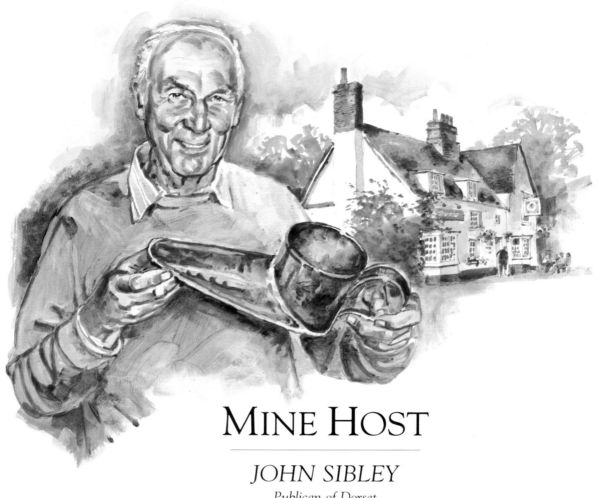

MINE HOST

JOHN SIBLEY
Publican of Dorset

As the long-serving landlord of a country pub, John Sibley gradually built up 'a good class trade', always knowing what sort of clientele he wanted. Even so, over the years he had to cope with some very awkward customers as well as accommodate a wide cross-section of society. Here he recalls some of the more extrovert people he encountered.

'One Sunday lunchtime I was serving in the lounge bar and it was very busy. This fellow came in with two tall and very attractive women and they had to sit in the far corner as there was only one small table left. But before they got there the man turned and shouted out: "Landlord, two double brandies," without so much as a please. How rude, I thought. He was obviously just trying to impress his female companions. So I ignored him completely and carried on serving.

'Eventually the man got to the bar, after he realised that no drinks were coming, and I could see that he was going to be an awkward cuss. He asked for the drinks again, plus a gin and tonic or something for himself, and I put them up. Then he said: "What's that?" pointing to the food on the bar. "Ham sandwiches," I replied. "Oh," he said, "I'll

48

have half a round." Unfortunately I had to say I was sorry, but that we only sold whole rounds. Jean made them fresh every Sunday morning and the last few there would soon be gone as they were so popular. And when they were gone, they were gone, as we always enjoyed sitting down promptly to our Sunday lunch. So I suggested that he took a whole round and left what he didn't want, and that's what he did, begrudgingly slamming down a fiver to pay for them. However, before I reached the till to get the change this half round of sandwiches whistled past my ear – and the bar went absolutely silent. So I calmly walked back and told him that he wouldn't get another drink here! People still talk about the incident today. You must always be friendly but firm in a pub; any sign of weakness and you're finished.

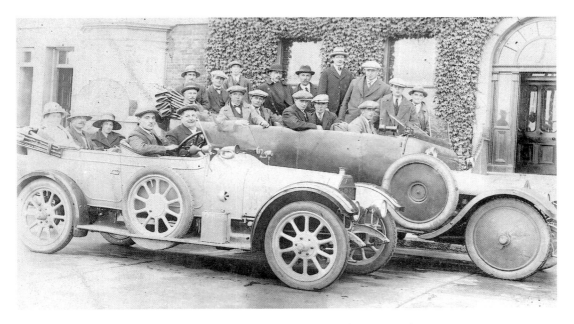

The ever-popular pub outing: here John's father (at the wheel) takes a group of customers on an outing

'We always had a lot of hunting people in, from the South Dorset Hunt whose kennels used to be behind the pub, and the Portman Hunt, and they usually tied their horses to the rail outside. But I remember one exception, when the so-called "squire of the village" rode up attired in full regalia; he saw this local by the door and said to him: "What are you doing there?" "Nothing, sir!" the man replied. So then the "squire" said: "Well, hold my horse and do nothing while I go in and have a . . . drink, then."

'Then there was this rector's wife, from a good Devon family, who used to come out in a taxi wearing men's clothes, with a suit and tie. She drank cherry brandy and occasionally let out a hunting cry which she claimed could be heard over a hundred yards through a copse! But she was a kind lady. One lunchtime these four council roadmen came in from their hedging and ditching and asked if they could eat their sandwiches in the corner, to which I agreed. "Who are they?" this lady asked; so I told her. "What a fine job they do," she said, and called out: "Give them all a pint of bitter – and make it your best!" And when they'd finished that, she bought them another, and another . . . Then Jean and I had to go to Bournemouth, and when we came back these four road-men were all laid out on the grass verge, fast asleep!

'In complete contrast were Mr King the pigman – who rode a tricycle for many years – and his wife, who came every evening, sat at each end of the bar and never said any-thing to each other all night.'

Mr King the pigman and his wife who sat at either end of the bar and never spoke

These incidents took place in the Dorset village of Sturminster Marshall, where John Sibley was landlord of the Black Horse from 1953 to 1973. But even before that he had had long experience of the licensed trade, as for thirty-six years his parents ran Wimborne's Albion Hotel, where John was born on 27 June 1923. The Albion was pre-viously called the New Inn, and it was here that George III had lunched on his way to Weymouth, where he took a dip from a bathing machine and started the big business of seaside resorts. As a boy, John vividly remembers how busy his parents were, 'father running the public bar to give the personality, and mother looking after the saloon'.

After attending Wimborne's Queen Elizabeth Grammar School, John took a tempo-rary shop job before conscription into the Navy in 1942, when he was eighteen. As a signal telegraphist, his tour of duty included serving on the Russian convoys, helping with the Normandy invasion, and in Hong Kong.

On his demobilisation in 1946, John returned to help his parents. One of their regular customers was the landlord of the Black Horse at Sturminster Marshall, who would come in for a drink on his way to the bank; his granddaughter was called Jean, and John married her in 1953. Her parents also kept a pub, the Red Lion at Blandford, where Jean was born, and they too became friends of the Sibleys. Furthermore, John's great aunt had the Old Bull and Bush when the famous song of that name came out; so the story goes.

As John says, 'pubs were very much in families then', so when he and Jean married they had the choice of the Albion or the Black Horse. They decided to take over from Jean's grandparents, William and Emma Bishop. Bill had taken the Black Horse in 1924 when bitter was 4d a pint. Because of ill health, he had given up his job as chauffeur and valet to Admiral Sir George Chetwode; in his younger days he had been Lady Chetwode's head stud-groom, in which connection it is perhaps worth mention that over his thirty years as landlord his weight increased from 6st 12lb to 14st 3lb! At the age of seventy-six he welcomed the chance to put his feet up, having worked hard without a break since he was nine; his only relaxation had been the occasional day's shooting or a visit to the races. Emma had trained as a tailoress, and many were the times she had taken out her needle and thread to replace a button for a customer. Bill loved talking about when, as a boy, he could buy an ounce of tobacco at Blandford for 3d and be handed a clay pipe and a box of matches to go with it. Some of his customers were great characters, too. One villager would drink fourteen pints at lunchtime and then go haymaking for the rest of the day!

The pub was the social centre of the village

The Black Horse

Bill Bishop was certainly one of Dorset's best known and most popular landlords, but the two who were licensees of the Black Horse before him were there even longer: the tenant immediately before Bill held the licence for fifty-two years, and his predecessor for sixty years. The pub's early history is sketchy; the current building is over 200 years old and retains many older features such as a cob wall (constructed of clay, gravel and straw in the seventeenth century), and is thought to have been built around an earlier pub, which burnt down. It is said to have been a free house on the Park estate, its front not facing the road but looking over the meadows to Sturminster Marshall.

So when John Sibley took over it was only the third time the pub had changed hands in 142 years. But the former landlords served very different days, and John envisaged considerable change for the Black Horse. Here he describes how he fared during his early days as licensee.

'Hall & Woodhouse of Blandford was such an old-fashioned family brewery. We even had to show our marriage certificate at the interview, whereas today some of these breweries don't even care if you're not married. Apparently, after we left Brigadier Woodhouse commented: "They're very young, but out of a good stable."

'We started on 4 December and soon realised that it was business seven days a week; you didn't even close on Christmas Day. At first we had to use a hand pump to draw fresh water in, and another to pump the waste water from the cesspit into the ditch! And Jean would scrub the flagstone floor on her hands and knees three times a week. At that time our till was an old Oxo tin!

'Jean's grandparents hadn't really wanted many customers – just enough to get by – as country pubs were more a way of life then; so we had to work the trade up. We had some idea of what we wanted, though we inherited a few customers who spoiled the image at first. One was Benny Hutchings, the pigman, who always came in with his filthy clothes and boots on – you could smell him coming before he opened the door – phew! Then he would sit down and rub his "Black Man" shag tobacco, all by the heat of an open fire, so you can imagine the pong that was generated! But when we pointed this out to him he simply said: "Ah, if you can smell that, you won't hurt!"

'We were determined to run a good, clean pub, somewhere you could bring your wife, so at first we had to bar one or two people for bad language. Occasionally a crowd of Teddy boys passed through, and when they said how quiet it was we soon encouraged them to go down the road. You can't mix oil and water – you've got to know what type of trade you want. And we were one of only two Hall & Woodhouse pubs which didn't have any fruit machines. But I did try to recreate the atmosphere of the old coaching days, and used a great many antique oil lamps as the lighting in a pub is so important. I also collected unusual objects such as an instrument for docking horses' tails, an implement for scraping the sweat off a horse, and leather tankards which were lined

Emma and Bill Bishop, mine hosts at the Black Horse in 1950. Note the bar snacks – two unwrapped pork pies on the shelf!

with pitch and made by the village cobbler for use by workers in the fields, where there was no fear of them being broken.

'I always called last orders about five or ten minutes before time, and dimmed the lights punctually. And we never entertained after hours. We came in with a good knowledge of pubs and were aware that as a rule, people couldn't be customers before time and friends after. Once this dentist we knew came in just after time and I relented. But when I served him a pint, in the dim lighting it happened to be the the tiniest bit short, and he had the cheek to say: "Fill it up." "Oh, no!" I said, "That's enough!" and I took the beer back. But after that he knew where to draw the line and we became friends.

'You were always conscious of under-age drinking, although in the old days it wasn't so much of a problem because you knew most people in a small community. However, I did once ask the dairyman's son if he was eighteen, only to discover that he was twenty-six and had two children! But in those days there would be a resident village policeman who was always well aware how you were running a pub; for us it was PC Willis who was a great support and would come immediately if there was any nonsense. He knew all the young people in the village, and their fathers, so there was little crime; if any youngster didn't behave he'd say: "I'll see your father about you!" and generally that was enough. He wasn't a great drinker, but he appreciated sitting by the fire on a cold night. His one great boast was that he had a truncheon with an American's tooth in it, one knocked out during the war.

'I never served gypsies, but there was one drove up the road who used to pinch a lot of daffodils grown on the local estate, then take the bus into Bournemouth to sell them. Poor old Willis could never catch him as there were two bus stops in the village and he was always at the wrong one!'

During John's time in the trade there were many changes in drink and drinking habits, generally reflecting national trends. Here he recalls some of the most significant:

'As a tenant, I got everything from Hall & Woodhouse, except cigarettes, which were sent from Player's to the local railway station. Our rent and overheads were very low at first, and mild beer was only about 8d a pint and ordinary bitter about 9d. We did charge 5d for a half, however, to make it more worthwhile and to save messing around with halfpennies. In the winter, especially at Christmas, we always had an old ale in little firkins – 4$\frac{1}{2}$ gallon casks. Unfortunately we were always up and down steps to the cellar because every pint had to be drawn from the barrels. And it was always a great deal of work looking after the beer. Each barrel had to be put up on "horsing" or "stilling" (wooden supports), to allow the sediment to settle. At the same time a hard spile would be knocked into the top, pushing through the bung. After a couple of days the hard spile would be replaced by a soft [porous] one to allow secondary fermentation to take place in the cask. This increased the alcohol while the carbon dioxide produced gave life to the beer and pressurised the cask, excess gas escaping through the porous spile. A tap was knocked into the barrel when the soft spile was inserted, and the latter was replaced by a second hard spile when the beer had stopped working. In those days here were no bottled lagers and nobody wanted cold beer then. It wasn't until the sixties that cooling systems and keg beer came in, with machines measuring out exact half pints. Now, fashion has gone full circle and people are wanting the real ales again.

'In the old days the only minerals sold were lemonade and ginger beer in stone jars, and London gin came in gallon stone jars. The biggest change in soft drinks came after World War II, when demand shot up because more girls started to go into pubs. The Britvic fruit juices became very popular, but the biggest success story was Babycham, introduced by Showerings. When we made out our weekly order we would just say: "Babycham, please!": there was no point in specifying a quantity because it was so popular, and the suppliers would send only what they could spare.

'Old English wines also became popular during our time, with our own specialities such as stirrup cup, Singapore sling, white lady, paradise and sidecar, as well as the non-alcoholic cocktail called "pussy foot". It was all a far cry from the old days of spit and sawdust.'

The social phenomenon which was largely responsible for transforming drinking habits was the mass production of the motor car, because many more town dwellers were then able to discover the delights of country pubs. Indeed, from the 1950s onwards no run in the country was complete without visiting the village inn with its old beams, many curios and its nostalgic image of yesteryear. As a result, many pubs became great meeting places. Being a former coaching inn and on a main road, the Black Horse attracted not only farmers, fieldsportsmen and other locals, but also people out for the day from nearby towns such as Poole and Bournemouth. To accommodate this change, the two ostler's cottages next to the Black Horse were demolished and a new car park

Pub and church: the centre of village life. It was not unknown for the 'back door' of the church to lead via a covered way to the back door of the pub next door

built on the site. The coach also played an important part in the development of pub trade, as John explains:

'Increasingly, people without cars went on trips in groups, and we were quick to notice all these Wessex coaches whizzing by, but none of them stopping at our place. So when I met one of the drivers in town I spoke to him about it, and he told me that we were on the black list. Apparently those coach drivers who had called at the pub in the old days had found there was nothing in it for them, and since then they all went elsewhere. So I invited him to call, and sure enough, two days later he came with a group of people. I gave him a thank-you drink, and later a bit of bread and cheese; and in the future if he came with a good load I gave him a packet of Player's, too. Word got about and it wasn't long before we had all the coaches coming in.

'Then the other coach companies started doing tours of Dorset and we did very well indeed in those early days. However, as more people bought cars the potential for more regular customers increased, and so the coach trade became a bad thing for us: it was all very well having a frantic period when a hundred people poured in from a couple of coaches, but these would be gone in half an hour and you'd be left with an empty car park because other visitors are often put off by coach crowds. This fact alone was bad for regular trade as, psychologically, the best advertisement a pub can have is a good

John had a good training for his role as publican with his parents at the Albion Hotel, Wimborne

number of cars on the forecourt. So we decided we had to get rid of the coaches, and stopped the perks – and the drivers blacklisted us overnight, just like pulling down a shutter! But we weren't sorry to see them go because it had become like a business. One young coach driver actually asked what it was worth if he brought a coachload in!'

The spread of the motor car also stimulated demand for inn food, as more and more people went out for the day and wanted to treat themselves. But unlike many other pubs, the Black Horse did not turn part of the building into a restaurant: instead it simply increased its range of bar snacks. Here John describes how they adapted:

'We didn't want to become one of these eating houses, as so many pubs have done, as a result losing all their character; nevertheless we had to provide more for our customers to persuade them to stay longer. In the early days we offered just the usual cheese sandwich, crisps and Miller's pork pies under a glass dome on the counter. Then Jean started to provide ham rolls made from meat cooked on the bone, and she was rightly proud of these. She was also very strict on hygiene and cleanliness – and was most upset on the occasion of a visit from an Egon Ronay representative. The rolls were under a tea towel to keep them fresh, and he asked: "What have you got there?" "Ham rolls," Jean replied. "Are they for sale, or have you put them to bed?" he said rudely!

'Next, Jean started to make and sell Scotch eggs, and a vicar also supplied us with chicken portions from his own birds; he needed the extra income and we did well out of it. Then the ploughman's lunch became really popular, and so we would always have Cheddar and Stilton on offer; we bought whole 60lb cheeses from the United Dairies in the village. They employed nearly everybody locally and claimed they were the biggest cheese factory in the world; although they have since closed down, and the site is now an industrial estate.'

John's greatest surprise did not come by car, however, nor even on foot: it came from above, and made front-page headlines in the *Dorset Herald*. John describes what happened:

'In June 1956 I was relaxing listening to the test match on the wireless when I heard some branches snap and saw something flapping about in the garden: this pilot had baled out and floated down through my chestnut tree onto just twelve square yards of lawn! "Where am I?" he asked. "In the back garden of the Black Horse, Sturminster Marshall," I replied. "Well, I couldn't have picked a better spot, could I? Give me a double brandy," he said. Luckily he was unhurt, and came in for a wash and a brush-up as well as a drink on the house.

'The man turned out to be Gordon "Chunky" Horne, a Vickers-Supermarine test pilot from Chilbolton airfield near Stockbridge. He had lost control of his Swift jet which had crashed into a field; meanwhile he had parachuted down, having to lift his legs to miss the high-tension electricity lines and my chimney. He also hoped he hadn't frightened our neighbour, who had been putting her washing out as he drifted past. Later, the joke

of the evening in the bar parlour was that although we relied on passing trade, this was the first time we had had a customer from *that* direction!

'When the jet crashed it had missed tractor man Jim Mouland by seconds, coming down in the path of his mowing machine. And 400 yards away, dairyman Bert Endicott was struck on the head by a piece of flying debris. He wasn't badly hurt, but all the farm workers had had a considerable fright!'

Another incident at the Black Horse worthy of mention occurred on the day John invited the local silver band in to play. By coincidence, the Salvation (Sally) Army band happened to stop and play outside, starting up at exactly the same moment as the silver band took its interval. When somebody went round with the hat to collect for the 'Sally' Army, the customers wrongly assumed that it was for the town's silver band which they had been enjoying so much – and not surprisingly, they gave very generously. As a result, when the collection for the silver band was made later, most people expressed surprise, protesting that they had already given.

Although the Black Horse did not then have a darts team, the game was very well supported in the pub, as was shove 'a'penny. Indeed, John vividly remembers that 'everybody wanted to play when this corker of a girl was scoring'!

Obviously, anybody taking on a pub must be gregarious and should like conversation; nevertheless all landlords run the risk of attracting the occasional bore.

'It's a bit like a hairdresser's business in that you have to listen to everybody's news and troubles, especially during very quiet periods in the winter. But Jean was always much better than me at chattering, and if the biggest bore had come in and was going on indefinitely about his swedes and tomatoes I soon left her to it and disappeared to watch TV!'

Pets could be a problem too, as John remembers only too well:

'Once someone brought in a young fox on a lead, although that was all right. It was the dogs wandering around the bar that were the real nuisance, scrounging for titbits and their wagging tails knocking glasses and things off low tables. The final straw was when one of the villagers' dogs cocked his leg on the furniture. Then they were banned!'

Today, John regrets many changes in the pub scene generally.

'The good pub always used to be the social centre of the village, though nowadays this is less often the case. We liked to provide a place where gentleman farmers, working farmers and farm workers could all mix happily together, with plenty of friendly banter. The important thing in the pub was to strike the right balance between firmness and fun. You had to lay down the law where necessary, but it was also essential to generate an atmosphere of enjoyment so that people wanted to come back. Certainly the law regarding excessive drinking and driving has changed pub drinking habits enormously, but who can argue against that? But a lot of the fun has gone along with the old characters, too; people like old "Zacker", who used to carry a sack around Wimborne, selling watercress.

'Jean always decorated the pub beautifully at Christmas, and we had a great time. Once one of our regulars went home on Christmas Eve, took his hat off and went to bed. But in the morning his wife said: "What on earth have you got on?" He was still wearing a paper hat from a cracker, and had been having such a good time he hadn't realised that he'd put his trilby on over the top of it!

'In the old days I could phone Edward Woodhouse at the brewery and have a chat about anything, and employers were friendly and approachable; but now the national trade is dominated by big business. Tenants have mostly been replaced by fixed-salary managers who have little incentive to cultivate regular custom, so most of the atmosphere has gone. To my mind, the good landlord should be closely involved in local activities; for example, I was president of the village football team for many years – the only disadvantage of this being that they kept winning cups and I had to fill them all up in celebration!'

When John and Jean retired they did not move far: they bought the thirty-acre farm next door, from a childless couple who wanted to go back to Sherborne. The place was in a 'hell of a state, with an old Jersey milking cow by the back door'. The previous owner had been a Black Horse customer for many years, and was a real character, as John recalls:

'Old Norman had this herd of Ayrshires, and he did everything at a snail's pace. When he brought the cows up for milking from fields along the road, they used to eat the next door neighbour's vegetables, of which the owner was very proud. One day in the bar this garden enthusiast plucked up courage and complained. But old Norman just looked up and in his wonderful Dorset accent said: " 'E don' wanna worry, Harold – they jus' be 'ungry!"

'Another time Norman was driving the cows along the road with the help of his little daughter. Suddenly this "toff" in a Jaguar car stopped, and complained as to this dangerous practice: " . . . the little girl on the road in charge of animals which are in *foal*". So old Norman paused a moment, and then said: "Well, I thought I be milkin' cows all these years. But if 'e says they be heavy in foal, they must be, and I must 'ave bin milkin' 'orses all these years." And so he went on, labouring the point in his particular manner.

'Norman used to buy packets of ten Player's Weights cigarettes, break them up and put the tobacco in his cherry pipe; and even this was always done in slow motion. One day a holidaymaker in the bar watched Norman take the papers off two cigarettes in his painfully slow way; a third was too much, however, and he couldn't contain his curiosity any longer, saying to Norman: "Excuse me, but isn't that an expensive way to smoke?" Norman paused in his unravelling, sat back and thought for a while, and then said: "Well, us farmers 'ave got to do somethin' with all our money, I suppose." '

John and Jean are still at the farm, raising a few beef cattle. They have extensively enlarged and modernised the house, but still have some of the many old pub artefacts which they had collected lovingly over the years, not least a rare copper mulling boot, used for heating ale. Also reminding them of the days when they were at the centre of village life is the view from their window, looking down on the Black Horse. It is a fitting place for the Sibleys to call time.

MUCH TO HIS CREDIT

JOHN GWYNNE

Shopkeeper of Breconshire (Powys)

It was wholly appropriate that 'J. Gwynne & Son' was voted the 'best village store' in 1994–5, having been the runner-up in a previous year, and John Gwynne assuredly deserves this acclaim having dispensed first-class service and extremely generous credit to the citizens of Talgarth for almost three-quarters of a century. Such benevolence is partly due to the fact that many Gwynne customers are farmers who have always been used to paying on account – most on a weekly, monthly or quarterly basis, but some still half-yearly! John even used to allow twelve months' credit, but was forced to rein back on such a lenient 'slate' as inflation accelerated and credit became tight all round. He admits: 'You could never ask regulars to pay up before time for risk of offending them.'

John Hugo Gwynne was born on 20 February 1921 at the Crescent Stores, Church Road, Talgarth, where his family had been in business since 1883. But his grandfather, William H. Gwynne, first set up shop two doors away in 1881, 'in the front room of Merlin House' about half a mile from the village centre.

In those days of relatively poor transport and communications, remote towns and

William Gwynne established the family business in 1881

villages such as Talgarth had to be much more self-sufficient, so most businesses had plenty of healthy competition. However, although his enterprise has come out on top, John regrets the demise of so many others: 'In Talgarth there used to be five petrol places, whereas now there are none. The ten pubs have been reduced to three, both cobblers have gone, and all the drapers and the greengrocers have closed; also the saddler's, the ironmonger's and two blacksmiths have gone; there is only one of three newsagents and one of three butchers left, and I'm the only grocer. Even the police station and court has closed.'

Yet John has never wanted to live anywhere else, and indeed he never did except during his wartime service in the RAF. Best of all, he likes the situation of Talgarth, which remains largely unspoilt in spite of the march of man and machines. Way back in Norman times the village was regarded as the capital of Breconshire; it was eloquently, but rather archaically described as follows in the *Talgarth Official Guide* issued just after World War II under the auspices of an enterprising Chamber of Trade:

'Population 2,000. Market day (farm produce): Fridays. Stock auctions: Mondays. Talgarth lies to the north-west of Crickhowell, from which place it is 12 miles distant, and 9½ miles from Brecon. It is situated at the foot of Parc Hill, a spur of the Black Mountains, at an altitude of 500 feet above sea-level. Nearby is the grand range of the Brecknock Beacons, with the rolling uplands of Mynydd Eppynt on the other side. Its scenic charms, its healthfulness and the varied beauties and interests of its surroundings make it an ideal centre for a quiet holiday.

'Let not the term "Black Mountains" give the reader a wrong impression. Black, after all, is useful as a foil and a background, and the range which shows to such advantage from Talgarth only looks black under certain atmospheric conditions, and from certain angles. On a clear summer day, and from a distance, the range is rather purple than black. Although for the most part built of stone, and of considerable antiquity, Talgarth is bright and cheerful. The air is mild but not humid, the rainfall is moderate, there are plentiful supplies of sunshine, and shelter from cold winds. Talgarth is, therefore, recommended by the medical profession for people who are run down or in need of recuperation after severe illness.

'It is also emphatically a centre for the robust and energetic, especially if they accept the challenge thrown down by the hills and mountain heights, on which, of course, the airs are very exhilarating. Matters vital to health, such as a pure and abundant water supply, efficient sewerage, and good sanitary arrangements are in the hands of a vigilant Rural District Council.'

With such a thriving, close-knit community and surrounded by largely unspoilt countryside on all sides, Talgarth was a wonderful place for John to grow up in.

'I went to Talgarth School from the age of five until I was fourteen, and there were many more children then as families were bigger and not many people moved away to work. I had five brothers and two sisters and we used to have a lot of simple fun. Sometimes we tied cotton to a doorknocker or to a button to tap a window, but when the person came to the door there was no one there because we were hiding in the churchyard! But we didn't always get away with things.

'Once when I was twelve there was some real excitement, when a London businessman staying in the Tower Hotel had a nervous breakdown. He had a gun in his room, and when the police went to arrest him he fired at them. This went on for twelve hours, and six of us kids who stayed to watch for much longer than we should got the cane for being late for school.

'There were some real characters around in those days. One of them was "Lizzie-the-Crate" Evans, so called because she was always taking apples to market. One day when she was there, us kids blocked her front door right up with snow so she couldn't get in, and then she sent the police after us.

'Another colourful person was Tom Weale, and he was always known as "Tom who roasted the cat" because one day he didn't notice that his cat had crept into the oven while the door was open and he accidentally cooked the poor creature alive!'

At the Crescent Stores, John's grandfather rapidly set about expanding the business, specialising in home-cured hams, bacon and tea-blending. He was certainly not reticent in advertising his wares; his tea-wrapper proclaimed: 'Let others boast of sparkling wines and drinks of high degree, but give to me at any time a cup of Gwynne's tea.' With such a bold approach, it was not surprising that he

John's father (left) and grandfather (right) outside the old Crescent Stores, where John was born

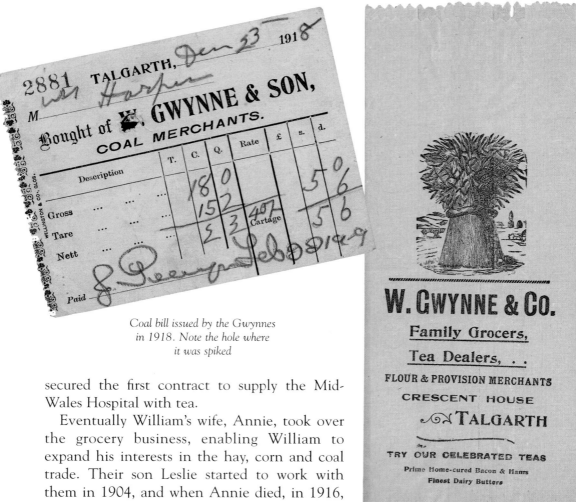

*Coal bill issued by the Gwynnes
in 1918. Note the hole where
it was spiked*

W. GWYNNE & CO.

Family Grocers,

Tea Dealers, . .

FLOUR & PROVISION MERCHANTS

CRESCENT HOUSE

TALGARTH

TRY OUR CELEBRATED TEAS

Prime Home-cured Bacon & Hams

Finest Dairy Butters

*The kind of tea bag used in John's
grandfather's day*

secured the first contract to supply the Mid-Wales Hospital with tea.

Eventually William's wife, Annie, took over the grocery business, enabling William to expand his interests in the hay, corn and coal trade. Their son Leslie started to work with them in 1904, and when Annie died, in 1916, Leslie's wife Jane took care of the shop. Leslie and Jane inherited the entire business when William died in 1934, aged 78. Leslie continued with the haulage work, his contracts including some for timber, one from the council to collect refuse, and others to deliver coal to schools. He also cut hay for local farmers, charging by the hour.

John started to work for the family at the age of twelve, while he was still at school. His first job was not with his parents, however, but with his aunt: she had a much bigger business, including a bakery, also in Talgarth. John describes those early days:

'As errand boy I delivered groceries in the carrier on my bike, but only around the village. The roads were pretty poor then as the council just used to put rough stones down, throw sand on top and roll it all in; so it wasn't surprising that I came off my bike a few times. Among the people I visited were the vicar, two doctors and the policeman, whose wife always used to give me a cup of tea. Most farmers came by horse and cart to get their own supplies, right up to the war. In those days it was nothing to see chickens and ducks in farmers' kitchens, and you still see pet lambs in some houses.

'I also helped aunty with house-to-house bread-van deliveries: she baked the bread, we took it round on a motor van and I got sixpence a week plus a meal or two.

'Another thing we used to do to earn extra money was pick hazelnuts and blackberries and sell them for a penny a pound to dealers called hucksters. These men also went round buying whinberries, mushrooms, holly, mistletoe, chickens, ducks, rabbits, hares, butter and eggs, which they took away to South Wales where they had a good market for most fresh produce in the industrial and coal-mining areas.

'I also used to blow the organ for a few bob a year. Grandad and my eldest brother were deacons in the chapel, and Grandad made us all go three times on Sunday, to 10.30am service, 2pm Sunday school and 6pm service. Many more people went to church then. In Talgarth we've always had a real mixture of denominations, including Congregationalists, Methodists and Baptists as well as the parish church, the Church of Wales. I've always been a Congregationalist, but my wife's a strong Methodist as she's from North Wales. It's common here for husbands and wives to go to different chapels.'

Following in his family's true entrepreneurial spirit, John only ever wanted to work in a shop. Therefore when he left school he went to work full-time in the shop which had been his aunt's, but which she had just sold; her name was retained above the door, however: D. L. Edwards. John recalls his three-year apprenticeship there:

'I had 2s 6d a week in the first year, 5s in the second and 7s 6d in the third. There was a manager, three of us boys, a man on the bread van and two bakers. What I found

The shop (left) in Talgarth Square, where John was apprenticed

the hardest was having to learn all the prices, as very few items were marked. It's all so precise now, with bar codes and computers, but I've always worked out the prices in my head. Among those I remember from the 1930s are 11½d for twenty Player's cigarettes, 7d a pound for cheese, 8d for a 4lb loaf of bread, 7½d for a 12oz tin of corned beef, and 11½d for an 8oz tin of red salmon. May butter was very cheap at only 10d a pound because it wasn't suitable for salting for winter use. Butter from the Irish Free State was always more popular than the local produce because it was cheaper.

'My first job in the morning was to sweep out, after which I had to fill the shelves. Then I'd weigh up the butter, marge, lard, currants, sultanas, raisins and that soft, moist brown sugar – I loved that! – in half-pounds and quarters. Peel and nutmegs were always whole. Salt came in blocks of 1½lb, but the farmers had much bigger blocks for salting pigs. Biscuits, flour and some tea were loose. Children used to come in after the broken

biscuits because they were cheaper, and farmers' wives used to make aprons out of the flour bags. New Zealand cheese used to come in 56lb rounds – two in a crate – and we had to take the cloths off them. Grapes, too, used to come in crates, in a kind of rough sawdust, and you had to dig down with your hands and pull them out. The banana crates often had big spiders in.

'We used to make grand window displays with sultanas, dried fruits, chocolates, flour, almonds, loose mixed peel and glacé cherries, which came in 7lb boxes and was really terrible sticky stuff to weigh out. In those days you used to keep things like Christmas cakes from year to year, but you can't do that now, as everything's dated.

'There were no fridges so I had to carry everything down to the cellar to keep it cool. There was a railway station here then, and every day we used to meet the train from Hereford at 10.30am to collect the sausages from Marsh & Baxters of Birmingham. They came on the passenger train, although less perishable items were quite all right on the goods train.

'We ordered most things from all the commercial travellers who came round. Nowadays very few reps call, and those who do only come infrequently. Everything's done by phone, which is a shame, because you lose that personal touch. In the old days if you were a good customer a rep would look after you, and each company had its own man; but now each rep has to deal with huge conglomerates and most have too much to think about.

'As boys we always asked the travellers for samples of sweets. I liked Radiance toffees best, and those slabs of Sharp's toffee, which we broke up and sold by the quarter.'

During the 1920s a very good produce market was held every Friday in Talgarth Market Hall, which was always full, with six or seven hucksters present. John remembers: 'Most of them came from Merthyr; they would buy all they could get, and then use the GWR and LMS railways to take it all home. In the 1930s the market went down to just three hucksters and they used road transport. After the war the market closed, and now the hall is empty; but we hope to start a youth club there.'

Today, John regrets the decline in Talgarth's community spirit:

'Things have changed for the worse, mainly due to people having cars. A lot of people have moved into Talgarth and quite a few commute long distances daily. Some have second homes and smallholdings in and around Talgarth, and only come here from London at the weekends for peace and quiet and the beautiful surroundings; but most are easy to get on with. At one time there were many more people on the land, and most stayed in the village so that everybody knew each other really well; but now there is so much machinery they are not needed. The main employers here are Bronllys Hospital and the Mid-Wales Mental Hospital, though the latter is due to close in 1998.

'There used to be many more local activities. For example, the harvest festivals used to be packed out, and we always used to have a good football team, and every year one of the farms held a "tea fight" and sports. The August show was always very popular, with horses, cattle, sheep and pigs penned on the football field. Before Talgarth's stock market was built all the stock was sold on the street. There also used to be a horse fair every May and November, which always attracted quite a few gypsies. They would come round the shop asking for dry [waste] cheese, and fat bacon to go with a rabbit.'

Rabbit was also a popular dish with the Talgarth residents, often being stewed. John recalls: 'There used to be many more roasts, and it was all joints, but now it's all stewing meat and chops sold. One of our favourite meals was a big roly-poly pudding with apples, sultanas and fruit in and boiled in a towel. Also popular were traditional Welsh cakes cooked on a hot plate.'

In 1942 John was called up and became an LAC despatch rider in the RAF, serving all over Europe. He admits: 'It was a great change for me and nearly broke my heart at first, until I paired up. Once I lost my way in Belgium and ended up at the front. I very soon made my way back! Another occasion I remember was when I was going into the Churchill Club in Berlin and bumped into my brother, an Army corporal in the stores. We were so surprised to see each other!'

John's father died in 1945 aged forty-seven, having been wounded in World War I. Soon after that John returned home to help his mother with the shop, and in 1946 he bought the Crescent Stores from her. He recalls:

'I had to buy the shop from Mum as we had a big family and there couldn't be any favouritism. Fortunately none of the local buildings had been damaged during hostilities and there were only a couple of bomb craters on the mountain; in fact Talgarth seemed almost unchanged after the war. There had been a lot of evacuees in the village, however, and some still call here. Homecoming parties were held in the town hall, and each serviceman returning was given a cheque from a special fund raised locally. When Father returned from World War I he was given a gold pendant, inscribed "Talgarth 1914–18". Nowadays my wife wears it on a chain.'

In the 1950s John rented a greengrocer's shop in Bell Street, which his mother ran and soon established as one of the best florist shops in the

The village shop in the 1930s: a real Aladdin's cave

area. Both businesses flourished, and John began to look for larger premises. Then, in April 1957, John fulfilled a lifetime ambition when he bought – 'for about £2,500' – the shop in which he had been apprenticed, D. L. Edwards. The new premises were much better placed, being close to Talgarth Square, although only two doors away from the largest grocery outlet in the village. But John was quite undeterred by the competition and was able to devote much of his energy to the new shop while his wife, Eunice, looked after Crescent Stores. When the Bell Street shop was closed in 1961 the fruit and vegetable trade was transferred to the new store, where John now employed three full-time staff. Eunice continued to run Crescent Stores.

But not everything went smoothly throughout this period. One day in 1954 when John was out delivering on his bike, poor Eunice sliced off two fingers in the bacon cutter. She remembers it well: 'It was the longest day of the year and they were cutting the grass in the churchyard. We called the doctor in and I was taken by car to Brecon hospital. The doctor joked: "Didn't you have enough bacon for the customers?" but it was the worst pain I ever had.' Sadly, at the time there was no chance of having the fingers sewn back on.

While most customers appreciated the Gwynnes' first-class service and remained loyal after a change of premises, there were always a few awkward ones. John himself has never actually been attacked, although one day he did have to part two men who were fighting in the shop itself. 'They'd been drinking, and were using filthy language. One woman used to have fits in the shop, and then there was the old lady who always came in just fifteen minutes before late closing, at a quarter to seven on Saturday, and I had to stay on late to take her order up on my bike. I used to curse her all right! We still get some customers who are always moanin' and groanin', but you just have to grin and bear it.'

During 1967 John chose to join the voluntary symbol group known as Mace. In the same year his son Leslie, who used to help out in the shop after school, started training for the business, enrolling at the College for the Distributive Trades in London. Twelve months later he returned with many new ideas; he became a partner in the business and in 1969 persuaded his father to buy an ailing shop in Talgarth Square, the site of the present store. John paid only £2,000 for this large and prominent building, 'because I was a Talgarth boy and an ex-serviceman. The first thing I did was change the name from "Evans The Stores"!' Their wholesalers helped with the launch, providing special offers which included butter at 2s 11d a pound, Brooke Bond tea at 1s 4d a quarter and lard at 5$\frac{1}{2}$d per packet. Ennig Stores was then sold and became a chemist's shop.

In 1970 many local people were alarmed when the Gwynnes revolutionised their store by turning it into a self-service shop. The older folk in particular were not at all keen on the idea, saying that it felt as if someone very important had died; but gradually they accepted it. Later the store was expanded and new lines were introduced, such as pre-packed fruit and vegetables, wines and spirits and locally baked bread, these being among the most popular items. However, with rapidly improving communications and transport, customers were becoming more price-conscious, so it was important to remain competitive by stocking Mace's own-brand products.

Yet further expansion into adjoining premises – first into what had been a separate bakery and confectionery, and then into a bank which had closed down – was encouraged by the growth in tourist trade, as increasingly mobile holidaymakers discovered the delights of the Brecon Beacons. Today the tourist trade remains strong, Germans and Dutch ('because of the mountains!') being the most frequent overseas customers. John does regret that being in a national park has severely restricted his development of the buildings, but in 1995 the authority did provide 50 per cent (£10,000) of the cost of restoring the shop front to more traditional style.

Previous shop fronts have seen excitement on at least two occasions. John recalls: 'One lady coming down the hill put her foot on the accelerator instead of the brake and shot through the window, and another time a chap did the same thing with an automatic.' Luckily no one was hurt on either occasion.

The only time that John was unable to continue his excellent delivery service to outlying areas – a service which has been truly appreciated by local farmers – was for two days during the great snow of 1947. Fortunately Talgarth had a local baker and a milkman who could keep people in the immediate vicinity supplied. Today the Gwynnes still offer a free delivery service to houses and farms up to about ten miles away, employing a van driver for three days a week. Such personal service, and the provision of quality products, have become even more important in retaining customer loyalty as cheap superstores have enticed many people to travel long distances to shop.

During John's lifetime little Welsh has been spoken in Talgarth, and in fact John himself cannot speak the language; but coming from North Wales, Eunice can, and she is always on hand to deal with the few older customers who prefer the native tongue.

Today the Gwynnes continue to offer quality service, yet they remain at the forefront of change. Where John once stacked soda-water syphons with a returnable 7s 6d deposit, popular wines from all over the world now fill the shelves. Along with chocolate, these new drinks are eagerly bought by customers who call regularly for their National Lottery tickets, resulting in an initial 10 per cent increase in turnover!

John still works hard, but now, with the support of his family and staff, he regularly takes time off to go to the races; he has a quarter share in the horse Treasure Again which has had some significant wins. His fine home, beautifully situated on the outskirts of Talgarth, contains many mementoes reflecting his passion for the Turf. It's all a far cry from the days when 'living above the shop your house was never your own, and friends were always coming in late having forgotten to buy something for supper or breakfast.'

Supplementary clothing and ration books which the Gwynnes handled

OUT OF AFRICA

ALICE MURNANE

Dispensing Doctor of County Meath, Ireland

Alice Murnane has undoubtedly always been a remarkably forceful lady; she grew up with a revolver in her hand, shot a crocodile, gained three university degrees in the days when most women remained housebound, ran a farm, practised general medicine long before penicillin, stitched wounds, set broken bones, delivered babies, pulled innumerable teeth and made house calls on horseback. At ninety-three she not only still enjoys a smoke and a tipple, but also remains active and interested in most aspects of modern life. But then she does put poteen in her Christmas pudding!

Christened Alice Irene Coster, this remarkable lady was born on 6 December 1903 at Bloemfontein in the Orange Free State, South Africa, where her parents met. Her father, whom she describes as 'very English', went out to the colony aged nineteen. He was in the land survey department of the Civil Service, then administered from London, but became disillusioned with 'pen-pushing' and decided to try his luck at prospecting for diamonds and panning for gold. Alice's mother – 'very Irish' – was equally adventurous and went out with the Queen Alexandra nurses to care for the troops during the Boer War.

Alice was always an inquisitive and independent child, at the age of twelve already studying Darwin's *Origin of Species*; indeed, South Africa's great outdoors provided the ideal nursery for a budding scientist, as Alice recalls:

'We lived in an area of semi-desert and it was all red soil, in complete contrast to Ireland's green. If it did rain, a marvellous thing happened: overnight the plants not only shot up, but bloomed, and the whole veldt was covered in colour.

'My brother and I played on the corrugated iron roof of our red-brick bungalow, but our hard shoes on the iron made an awful noise. This made the Dutch woman who lived next door very angry and one day she took out her gun and said: "If you don't get down I'll shoot you".

'When I was only eleven Father taught me how to use a Colt revolver, which I thought was great. He said that it was necessary for a white woman in Africa.'

Alice attended a Catholic convent school in Bloemfontein, but then her mother decided that an Irish education would be a good idea. The family had little money to spare but a brother of Alice's mother, a bachelor doctor in the British Royal Army Medical Corps, was very kind to them and financed the move. He had joined the RAMC because 'it was just about the only job a doctor could get in those days, when there were hardly any dispensing doctors worth talking about and they were very poorly paid'.

Alice, aged twelve

So at the age of sixteen, Alice was despatched to Loreto Abbey School, Rathfarnham, County Dublin. It took three weeks to reach Ireland, and for Alice this was 'an astonishing change'. In South Africa, when she looked at the horizon she saw 'nothing but this reddish ground going on for ever; water rationing was normal and dead cows were a common sight beside the road.' But in Ireland the fields were small, water was abundant, everything was green and lush and the cattle were fat.

On leaving school Alice returned to South Africa, where she read zoology at Grey University, Bloemfontein, now called the University of the Orange Free State. She clearly remembers what a formidable challenge this presented.

'Up to then there were only Afrikaner students there and I was one of only five English-speaking girls allowed in for the first time. We had English texts but all the lectures were still in Afrikaans so we had to work extra hard; but we still came top of everything. The Boers were still very anti-British after the Boer War.'

There was further excitement when Alice joined other students on a zoology trip to Portuguese East Africa.

'Our luggage had been delayed so we had to stop on the Transvaal border. The station master put us up in Kaffir huts, which were wonderfully cool in summer. Their floors were made of mud and dung, but you'd never know it. We went down to bathe in the Limpopo and then the station master came rushing out shouting: "Get out, get out; you'll get bilharzia[sis] [a chronic disease produced by a parasitic flatworm]".

'He took me up-river and asked if I would like to use a rifle; so I did. There were all these hippos in the river and he told me to have a go at a crocodile on the opposite bank. I fired, but the croc never moved, so I was never sure whether it was dead or just didn't care!'

On completing her BSc, Alice became assistant to one of the professors at Grey University, where she went on to take an MSc in zoology. Her thesis was concerned with leeches, but at the time she had no idea that one day she would become a doctor and that, coincidentally, one of the disused pieces of medical equipment in her surgery would be a leeches jar, from the old days of blood-taking.

Alice's army uncle, however, suggested that she should follow his example and study medicine back in Ireland, which she did. At this time, Alice's mother was increasingly anti-British, having first joined an Irish league in South Africa. She also became active in fighting for the emancipation of women in Ireland. Much of her dissatisfaction stemmed from the fact that her people had once been evicted from their Irish farm by landowners of Anglo-Norman descent, for advocating better wages for poor people. Her rebelliousness was fuelled by the unrest generated by the Easter Rising of 1916 and eventually contributed both to separation from her husband, who remained in South Africa, and to her falling out with her future son-in-law, whom she considered put ideas into Alice's head. At first 23-year-old Alice went to Trinity College, but when a friend of her uncle's expressed surprise at her attending a Protestant university, she transferred to UCD. On gaining her medical degree she worked briefly as a junior doctor at Vincent's Hospital, in Dublin.

In 1934 Alice married Doctor Jack (John Ignacious) Murnane; Jack had taken up medicine after spending two years in Rome training to become a priest, and was twenty-five years her senior. But then it was common for Irishmen to marry much younger women; maybe they suddenly decided they wanted children, or perhaps they needed help when all their sisters had left home and were no longer available to work on their farms.

Jack was the medical officer for the Dunsany and Kilmessan Dispensary District and was based in the tiny hamlet of Belper, on County Meath's Tara Hill, a place steeped in Irish legend and history. As well as the surgery and gate lodge dispensary at his home, he had surgeries at Kilmessan and Kilmoon.

(top) Medical student Alice Murnane (front, second from right) in Dublin; (above) Alice was the only female in this group of graduates in medicine at University College Dublin

Alice became Jack's assistant as soon as she moved to Belper, and quickly discovered how self-sufficient they had to be. Her many tasks included growing vegetables, injecting sheep and cattle, milking two cows, making butter and keeping bees. She often had a dozen lambs indoors, and even then it was usual practice to warm up a weak one in the bottom oven of the Aga. But you need to put them in a box, or put a blanket between them and the wall of the oven or they will singe. Jack, too, was very adaptable and once treated a herd of cows for diarrhoea!

Although Dublin was only about nineteen miles away, transport was still very slow and there were no emergency and support services like those of today, so only the most serious cases were sent to hospital. Alice recalls the many difficulties of those early days:

'People weren't too keen on having a lady doctor; in fact there were only two of us in County Meath then. Furthermore, those who came to the dispensary looked on me with great suspicion as I was someone they'd never even seen before, an outsider coming into a close-knit community.

'Our salary from the county council's board of guardians was only about £200 a year. Generally there were no free medicines except to sick patients, but the poor got free medical attendance and medicines under a ticket system. The better off were supposed to pay, but if Jack thought you couldn't afford it he didn't bother you. Some farmers paid in sovereigns because they liked to save in gold rather than put their money in the bank, and others paid in kind with things such as turkeys and vegetables. But Lord Dunsany was very generous and paid a regular salary to Jack as there were about fifty servants to care for at his castle.

'Trains were the only means of public transport until buses started in the 1920s, and none of the roads were tarred until 1929. Most people came to our weekly surgeries by horse and cart, on horseback or on foot. Horace Plunkett had imported a car, a De Dion Bouton, before World War I, and this was thought to be not only the first car in the area but the first in the country. But when I came, when you went to Dunsany church the only cars you'd see parked outside were Jack's and the priest's, who used to have a bike, too. There'd also be about eight to ten traps, the horses tethered in the chapel shed, and scores of bicycles lined up along the school wall. In about 1934 I was given my first car – a baby Austin with mica windows and a soft top – by the son of Lord Fingall of Killeen Castle.

'Jack hunted twice a week with the Meath Foxhounds and the Ward Staghounds, as Lord Fingall said that was the best way to get to know people. The horses were also useful for going to surgeries and visiting patients in more remote areas, such as Kilmoon. In snowy weather it was much quicker to go direct across country on horseback, especially as the land was not all divided by barbed wire then. So we had special panniers

made for our equipment and I, too, started to ride and hunt. Mostly it was only upper class ladies who went hunting then, but I managed to keep on most of the time as I was pretty tough, having played a lot of hockey and climbed Table Mountain! The important thing was to know *how* to fall off. Before then I'd only ever ridden an African Basuto pony which only ambles and never runs or even trots, but Jack simply put me up on a big horse and told me not to look down. Then, as now, farmers would cross a cart mare with a Thoroughbred to get a good hunter.

'Petrol rationing made life very difficult during World War II; we were limited to sixteen gallons a month, which didn't get us very far. To save fuel I bought a two-stroke motorbike on which to make calls, but I often broke down and ended up pushing. Fortunately some kind farmer usually came along, heaved my motorbike up onto his horse and cart and took me home.

'Some patients were very good to us and gave us petrol coupons and tyres, which were extremely hard to come by – where they got them from we never knew! Another patient I remember used to go on real "benders" and Jack would confiscate his clothes to prevent him going out. But one day his wife phoned up and said: "That's no use, come quickly!" So Jack went over, and there was the man walking to the pub in his nightshirt, barefoot in the pouring rain but with his umbrella up!

'We had to cope with every type of emergency, from stitching a face wound due to a horse kick to setting broken bones and delivering babies. We always carried a selection of splints as well as a special accident bag and a maternity bag. I did a lot of the early-morning work as Jack wasn't an early riser. If there was a maternity case he'd stay dressed till three in the morning, as he'd say there wasn't any point in getting undressed then dressed again. All midwifery in the district was done by Jack, the local midwife and me. All the women had rickety pelvises – due to a lack of vitamin D as children – but no case disturbed Jack: he could deliver a baby whatever the state of the mother.

'Once we took a visiting friend to the Abbey Theatre, but a man suddenly came on stage and said: "Is there a Doctor Murnane in the house?" So we had to go back as Mrs O'Sullivan was having twins, and arrived to find the other people there were very worried about her; Jack told them he would have to operate, which concerned them even more. "But you'll kill her," they said. "Well, she'll die if we don't," Jack replied.

'We had a very wide range of surgical and other instruments, including special ones for pulling each kind of tooth. A knife grinder, who walked round with his equipment in a pram, used to stop by to sharpen our blades.'

The Murnanes' main occupation was making up medicines, since the only other chemist in the area was in Dunshaughlin. They also made up ointments for horses. All the ingredients came in jars from Dublin and had to be collected by horse and cart from Kilmessan station. Furthermore, Alice undertook all the testing of urine, work now done by a centralised laboratory service.

In those days, before scientifically formulated modern medicines became widely available, there was often little the doctor could do for a patient other than alleviate his or her pain, as Alice clearly remembers:

The De Dion Bouton, which was one of the earliest types of car to be seen in the British Isles

'Really I just learnt as I went along, as I'd always done. I'll never forget when I gave my first anaesthetic, as an assistant. I was so concerned to do the right thing I put myself out as well as the patient, when I dripped ether onto her face mask – it was half an hour before I came to! I think it gave me as great a shock as the time when I took snuff at a wake.* It was the first time I'd seen it, and everybody would take a pinch as they went in.

'Diptheria was very common and there was nothing effective to combat it. Every day we had to remove the white fuzz off a patient's tonsils, to stop him choking. Polio was common, and tuberculosis was another big problem, when all the sufferer could do was wait to die. Most of the old folks of, say, between fifty and seventy-five died of pneumonia; although it was often known as "the old man's friend" because it put an end to a lot of suffering. The women died of it too, but they were mostly susceptible because they were worn out through hard work. All we could do for a pneumonia sufferer was slap a poultice on his chest.

'Colds were very common, the only antidotes being aspirin and cough medicine. There was no awareness of nutrition then, and there were many more boils and tonsular abscesses.** However, there were no cot deaths: babies were always laid on their backs in those days and I for one always knew that putting them on their face was fatal.

'When I started in practice a considerable amount of superstition lingered on; for example some people believed that warts would disappear if you tied a rag on a tree. But, with better education, traditional mistrust of doctors rapidly disappeared and greatly improved communications did away with much need for self-help.

'A doctor's life was made considerably easier by the introduction of sulphonamides [substances able to prevent the multiplication of some pathogenic bacteria], but it was the introduction of penicillin that put an end to most of the long-established ailments. [Penicillin was discovered in 1928, although a method of producing the volatile drug was not perfected until 1939.] Now, however, I consider that people are living too long. Jack had a stroke and it took him seven weeks to die, and one of the nuns commented: "That's modern medicine for you." I hope nobody bothers too much with me; I want to be left to die when my turn comes.'

*The wake used to be a much more important part of Irish life, with relatives and friends sitting around the body chatting over cups of tea. Whiskey, tobacco and meals were very often provided, but it was very expensive for the bereaved.

**Many of the medical problems stemmed from poor living conditions such as dampness and overcrowding, as well as very restricted diet, often the result of poverty.

Alice did all she could to alleviate the poverty among her patients, and this concern was the driving force behind her attitude to birth control.

'When there was no modern contraception available I introduced the women round about to the rhythm theory – contraception by avoiding sexual intercourse near times of ovulation – worked out in Japan and which I had read up about. I just felt so sorry for all these women who came into the dispensary with a lot of children. Of course, some of them went straight down and told the priest, in confession, all about this carry-on, and next time he saw me he looked at me very strangely, though he never said a word! Anyway, I didn't care what he thought, as the health of these women was more important. I used the method myself, too.

'Having so many children was quite ridiculous when most people earned so little. The man who did most of our work and tended our horses earned only 15s a week; we also had a cook and a housemaid, and they received only £1 a week each, although we fed them like fighting cocks. They liked coming to us because people used to say that working at the doctor's made matrimony a certainty. And sure enough, I married them all off!'

Over the years Alice encountered many great characters and some very distinguished people, not least Edward Plunkett, the 18th Lord Dunsany. Here Alice recalls this well-known novelist and playwright:

The examination of patients often had to be carried out in less-than-perfect conditions

'As Jack was his doctor he always had the road between us cleared of snow as quickly as possible; his men would rig up a V-shaped plough made of two great bars of wood bolted at one end, which was dragged by two horses and would push the snow to both sides.

'During World War II there were a great many British airmen interned at The Curragh, and Dunsany considered that if he and his supporters could free them they could drive them back over the border into Northern Ireland, with the help of Jack's car and petrol. They worked out a code, and on the nights that Jack received a note saying "Please come, I have diarrhoea" he was to go to the castle. In the end he went down once or twice but there were no men there, and it turned out that it was only one of his friends playing games. Nevertheless they had a whale of a time when they all got together. Every Wednesday Jack used to drive Dunsany to Dublin, partly so that he could visit the British embassy.

'Dunsany was a very interesting man. He could talk for an hour on a single word in the English language, yet hold you spellbound. He was also great fun. The children used to go up to his drawing room after tea and he'd build a tower of bricks on this lovely carpet and light a fire under it; when the smoke came out of the top he poured water down into it. He must have had something underneath to protect the carpet, but we didn't notice it, and all the children were fascinated by this. I still have all Lord Dunsany's books, which he signed for me.'

Jack had not signed any contract of employment for the county council and so they could not evict him from their property; in fact he chose to continue working until he was seventy, and Alice continued to do locums for many years after that. Eventually, however, they bought a farm at nearby Roestown, Dunshaughlin; Alice now lives in the house which they had built at Drumree, Leishmanstown, Jack having died before it was completed, in 1969.

Things have certainly changed a great deal during Alice's many years within the shadow of Tara. Long gone are the days when corncrakes were so plentiful that they kept her awake at night with their rasping call. Most of the partridges have vanished, along with the great flocks of golden plover, a bird which Alice used to shoot in the 1930s, from a hide in the middle of a field. However, it was not the pressure of sport that brought about the demise of so much wildlife, but the destruction of so much habitat caused by new agricultural practices.

Human lives have changed dramatically, too. The combined stores and post office (now closed) at Dunsany where Alice used to shop for most things, was where Horace Plunkett started the hugely successful Co-operative movement. Also the district's population has soared as commuting has become so easy and many city-bred folk now prefer to live in the country. But there has been much emigration as well as immigration: during the early part of this century most of the young people born on Alice's round would have been content to spend the rest of their lives locally, working on the land, many of them hoping and expecting to find employment on the great estates of Dunsany and Killeen. Dublin might as well have been a million miles away. But today most of the youngsters look to the capital, now only half an hour away by car, as well as across the sea to Europe – their 'village' of the future. And not only do they have new horizons and new aspirations, but also greatly improved health and vigour, brought about by a much improved standard of living and accessibility to sophisticated medical care.

Well-earned retirement after decades of doctoring

Sturdy Savages

We have two gangs or hordes of gypsies which infest the south and west of England, and come round in their circuit two or three times a year. One of these tribes calls itself by the noble name of Stanley; of which I have nothing particular to say; but the other is distinguished by an appellative somewhat remarkable. As far as their harsh gibberish can be understood, they seem to say that the name of their clan is Curleople.

With regard to these peculiar people, one thing is very remarkable, and especially as they come from warmer climates; and that is, that while other beggars lodge in barns, stables and cow-houses, these sturdy savages seem to pride themselves in braving the severities of winter, and in living *sub dio* the whole year round. Last September was as wet a month as ever was known; and yet during those deluges did a young gypsy girl lie in the midst of one of our hop-gardens, on the cold ground, with nothing over her but a piece of blanket extended on a few

HARVEST-HOME.

hazel-rods bent hoop-fashion, and stuck into the earth at each end, in circumstances too trying for a cow in the same condition; yet within this garden there was a large hop-kiln, into the chambers of which she might have retired, had she thought shelter an object worthy of her attention.

Violent Storm

On June 5th, 1784, the thermometer being at noon at 70, the barometer at 29.65 and the wind north, I observed a blue mist, smelling strongly of sulphur, hanging along our sloping woods, and seeming to indicate that thunder was at hand. I was called in about two in the afternoon, and so missed seeing the gathering of the clouds in the north; which they who were abroad assured me had something uncommon in appearance. At about a quarter after two the storm began in the parish of Hartley, moving slowly from north to south; and from thence it came over Norton-farm, and so to Grange-farm, both in this parish. It began with vast drops of rain, which were soon succeeded by round hail, and then by convex pieces of ice, which measured three inches in girth. Had it been as extensive as it was violent, and of any continuance (for it was very short), it must have ravaged all the neighbourhood. In the parish of Hartley it did some damage to one farm; but Norton, which lay in the centre of the storm, was greatly injured; as was Grange, which lay next to it. It did but just reach to the middle of the village, where the hail broke my north windows, and all my garden-lights and hand-glasses, and many of my neighbours' windows. The extent of the storm was about two miles in length and one in breadth. We were just sitting down to dinner; but were soon diverted from our repast by the clattering of tiles and the jingling of glass. There fell at the same time prodigious torrents of rain on the farms above-mentioned, which occasioned a flood as violent as it was sudden; doing great damage to the meadows and fallows, by deluging the one and washing away the soil of the other. The hollow lane towards Alton was so torn and disordered as not to be passable till mended, rocks being removed that weighed two hundred-weight. Those that saw the effect which the great hail had on ponds and pools say that the dashing of the water made an extraordinary appearance, the froth and spray standing up in the air three feet above the surface. The rushing and roaring of the hail, as it approached, was truly tremendous.

Crickets on the Hearth

The house-cricket resides altogether within our dwellings, intruding itself upon our notice whether we will or no. The species delights in new-built houses, being, like the spider, pleased with the moisture of the walls; and besides, the softness of the mortar enables them to burrow and mine between the joints of the bricks or stones, and to open communications from one room to another. They are particularly fond of bakers' ovens, on account of their perpetual warmth.

Tender insects that live abroad either enjoy only the short period of one summer, or else doze away the cold, uncomfortable months in profound slumbers; but these, residing as it were, in a torrid zone, are always alert and merry – a good Christmas fire is to them like the heat of the dog-days. Though they are frequently heard by day, yet is their natural time of motion only in the night. As soon as it grows dusk, the chirping increases, and they come running forth, and are from the size of a flea to that of their full stature. As one should suppose, from the burning atmosphere which they inhabit, they are a thirsty race, and show a great propensity for liquids, being found frequently drowned in pans of water, milk, broth, or the like. Whatever is moist they affect; and therefore often gnaw holes in wet woollen stockings and aprons that are hung to the fire; they are the housewife's barometer, foretelling her when it will rain, and are prognostic sometimes, she thinks, of ill or good luck, of the death of a near relation, or the approach of an absent lover. By being the constant companions of her solitary hours they naturally become the objects of her superstition. These crickets are not only very thirsty, but very voracious; for they will eat the scummings of pots, and yeast, salt, and crumbs of bread, and any kitchen offal or sweepings.

When they increase to a great degree, as they did once in the house where I am now writing, they become noisome pests, flying into the candles, and dashing into people's faces; but may be blasted and destroyed by gunpowder discharged into their crevices and crannies. Their shrilling noise is occasioned by a brisk attrition of their wings. Cats catch hearth-crickets, and, playing with them as they do with mice, devour them. Crickets may be destroyed, like wasps, by phials half filled with beer, or any liquid, and set in their haunts; for being always eager to drink, they will crowd in till the bottles are full.

All extracts taken from *The Natural History of Selbourne*, 1789 by Gilbert White.

The Seventh Child

In Cornwall, the peasants and the miners believe that a seventh son can cure the king's evil by the touch. The mode of proceeding usually is to strike the part affected thrice gently, to blow upon it thrice, to repeat a form of words, and to give a perforated coin or some other object to be worn as an amulet. At Bristol, about forty years ago, there was a man who was always called 'Doctor', simply because he was the seventh son of a seventh son. The family of the Joneses of Muddfi, in Wales, is said to have pre- sented seven sons to each of many successive gener- ations, of whom the seventh son always became a doctor – apparently from a conviction that he had an inherited qualification to start with. In Ireland, the seventh son of a seventh son is believed to pos- sess prophetical as well as healing power. A few years ago, a Dublin shopkeeper, finding his errand- boy to be generally very dilatory in his duties, inquired into the cause, and found that, the boy being a seventh son of a seventh son, his services were often in requisition among the poorer neigh- bours, in a way that brought in a good many pieces

THE MORRIS-DANCERS.

of silver. Early in the present century, there was a man in Hampshire, the seventh son of a seventh son, who was consulted by the villagers as a doctor, and who carried about with him a collection of crutches and sticks, purporting to have once belonged to persons whom he had cured of lameness. Cases are not wanting, also, in which the seventh daughter is placed upon a similar pinnacle of greatness. In Scotland, the *spae wife*, or fortune-teller, frequently announces herself as the seventh daughter of a seventh daughter, to enhance her claims to prophetic power, Even so late as 1851, an inscription was seen on a window in Plymouth, denoting that a certain doctress was 'the third seventh daughter', which the world was probably intended to interpret as the seventh daughter of the seventh daughter of a seventh daughter.

No Puffing Permitted

Smoking was formerly forbidden among schoolmasters. In the rules of the school at Chigwell, founded in 1629, it was declared that 'the master must be a man of sound religion, neither Papist nor Puritan, of a grave behaviour, and sober and honest conversation, no tippler or haunter of alehouses, and no puffer of tobacco'.

Tips for the Teacher

There is a curious custom of old standing in Scotland, in connection with Candlemass Day (2 Feb). On that day it is, or lately was, an universal practice in that part of the island, for the children attending school to make small presents of money to their teachers. The master sits at his desk or table, exchanging for the moment his usual authoritative look for one of bland civility, and each child goes up in turn, and lays his offering down before him, the sum being generally proportioned to the abilities of the parents. Sixpence and a shilling are the most common sums in most schools; but some give half and whole crowns, and even more. The boy and girl who give most are respectively styled King and Queen. The children, being then dismissed for a holiday, proceed along the streets in a confused procession, carrying the King and Queen in state, exalted upon that seat formed of crossed hands. In some schools, it used to be customary for the teacher, on the conclusion of the offerings, to make a bowl of punch and regale each urchin with a glass to drink the King and Queen's health, and a biscuit. The latter part of the day was usually devoted to what was called the Candlemass bleeze, or blaze, namely, the conflagration of any piece of furze which might exist in their neighbourhood, or, were that wanting, of an artificial bonfire.

Resorting to Riddles

How our ancestors managed to pass the long winter evenings in the olden time, has never been satisfactorily explained. They had no new books, indeed few books of any kind, to read or talk about. Newspapers were unknown; a wandering beggar, minstrel, or pedler circulated the very small amount of news that was to be told. The innumerable subjects of interest that form our ordinary topics of conversation were then utterly unknown. So we can only conclude that our ancestors, like some semi-savage tribes at the present day, passed their spare hours in relating often-told stories, and exercised their wits in asking each other puzzling questions or riddles. Many copies of what we would now term riddle-books, are found in both the French and English collections of old manuscripts, and some were printed at an early period; one in English by Wynkyn de Worde, in 1511.

Poteen and St Patrick

Poteen, a favourite beverage in Ireland, is also said to have derived its name from St Patrick; he, according to legend, being the first who instructed the Irish in the art of distillation. This, however, is, to say the least, doubtful; the most authentic historians representing the saint as a very strict promoter of temperance, if not exactly a teetotaller. We read that in 445 he commanded his disciples to abstain from drink in the daytime, until the bell rang for vespers in the evening. One Coleman, though busily engaged in the severe labours of the field, exhausted with heat, fatigue, and intolerable thirst, obeyed so literally the injunction of his revered preceptor, that he refrained from indulging himself with one drop of water during a long sultry harvest day. But human endurance has its limits: when the vesper bell at last rang for evensong, Coleman dropped down dead – a martyr to thirst. Irishmen can well appreciate such a martyrdom; and the name of Coleman, to this day, is frequently cited, with the added epithet of *Stadhach* – the thirsty.

All extracts taken from *The Book of Days*, 1866 by Richard Chambers.

MINISTERING TO TWO FLOCKS

THE REVEREND FRED PENNINGTON

Priest and Farmer of Devon

During the first four decades of his remarkable life, farmer Fred Pennington often helped resuscitate weak, new-born lambs and piglets within the warmth of his farmhouse kitchen. But over the following forty years Fred ministered to a very different flock, when he became both priest and healer. Instead of instilling new life into animals with a drop of brandy and tender loving care, he increasingly helped sick and distressed people, revitalising both body and spirit through faith, hypnosis, the laying-on of hands and exorcism. Although now retired from the church, this exceptionally youthful octogenarian retains a healing ministry of international renown. Indeed, he has even helped members of the royal family. Yet this modest man remains very close to his country roots.

One of two brothers, Frederick William Pennington was born on 4 August 1911 in the parish of Hartland, North Devon, where his family have lived since 1550. Bordered by the Atlantic Ocean to the west and the Bristol Channel to the north, this relatively isolated area then had a very insular community, and farming there was always difficult in such a windswept quarter. But these factors produced very independent and caring people, always ready to help each other; and none more so than Fred. Now the parish has become a Mecca for holidaymakers who are attracted to the many coves and wild shoreline; but Fred loves it just the same.

Fred's birthplace was a little thatched cottage in the hamlet of Stoke, about a mile from Hartland village. For some years his father had been a gardener and his grandfather was the farm bailiff on Sir Lewis Stucley's Hartland Abbey estate. When Stucley died, grandad Pennington was offered the tenancy of Newton Farm, a mile south of Stoke and a mile west of Hartland village, and the family moved there in 1912.

At first, Fred was extremely reluctant to attend the village school because, like

Fred's grandfather and his sister at Newton Farm, Hartland; farming has always been difficult there because the peninsula is repeatedly windswept

many country children of the time, he had rarely come into contact with anyone except his relatives and neighbouring farm families. Suddenly to be thrust among a hundred or so strange and sometimes rough children, at a place which seemed many miles from home, was a daunting experience for a five-year-old who had made few relationships. Indeed, on his very first day at school Fred decided he'd had enough, so on the next two days he slipped away from his cousin who lived on a neighbouring farm and acted as Fred's escort to lessons. But Fred soon had to submit to his mother's will. He still recalls his schooldays in great detail:

'The school took children up to the age of fourteen and they all had to walk there – some as much as four miles – from the age of five. They would leave home on dark winter days to climb the steep cliff roads in howling south-westerly gales, and not get back until after dark. But no matter how far you walked, everyone had to do a half-hour's "drill" [PE] each morning, before starting lessons.

'There was only one small, water-heated radiator in each schoolroom, so in the winter we were often very cold. We carried our dinners in canvas bags slung across our shoulders, and by the time we reached school on a rainy morning our food was well soaked. We had to eat it standing around a cloakroom radiator, if we were strong enough to get near it, and the meal was washed down with cold water.

'A common breakfast before going to school was "kettle broth", made by breaking a slice of bread into a basin, adding a lump of butter, pepper and salt, then pouring on boiling water. We often had this before going to bed, too, if we had a cold.

'In those days it was rare to have a boy or girl at the school who had not been born in Hartland or a neighbouring parish. Consequently, we all spoke in our Devon dialect and it was often difficult to make ourselves understood to outsiders, or even to our teachers.

'Our main games were with marbles. On the way to and from school we played "followers-on", where one boy would throw a marble along the road as far as he could and still keep it in sight, while another boy would try to get his marble as close to that of the first boy as possible, so that he could "span" the two marbles. This meant touching one marble with his thumb and at the same time with the little finger of the same hand attempting to touch the second. If successful he could then claim his opponent's marble.

'In the second game, in the playground, a marble was thrown against the wall so that it rebounded a few feet away. A second boy repeated the exercise and tried to get his marble close enough to the first to span it. When he did the marble was his.

'In this way some boys built up quite a collection of marbles and to us our collections seemed very valuable. One boy called Stan had such a wide span that he always seemed to win everybody else's marbles. There was always, too, the boy who dealt in marbles and seemed to make a profit out of them. We could rarely afford to buy them even though they cost only a penny for about twenty. Some boys would try to cheat by baking marbles in an oven, so making them rebound more sharply from the stone, giving greater accuracy. These were called "stoneys" and there was always a careful examination of those to be used before each game began.

Loading hay onto the waggon; this photograph was taken at harvest-time in 1904

'Another game the older boys played was called "cats and dogs". It was something like modern baseball except that instead of a ball a piece of wood about six inches long and an inch thick was pitched to a boy holding a heavy stick some three feet long, and when the piece was struck it would spin at a terrific rate. The game was banned after a boy suffered a damaged eye and lost his sight.

'Another popular pastime we called "fox and hounds". This we played after dinner, before afternoon school. One boy would set off across the fields and after about ten minutes a dozen of the more energetic ones would give chase, shouting "eek, squeak, whistle or ollee [holler], else the little dug want volee [dog won't follow]". This sometimes took up to two hours, and then we didn't get back to school that day, which inevitably meant trouble the following day, with the cane or being kept in after school. Whenever possible, we arranged the "hunt" for a Friday, hoping that the teacher would forget the incident by the following Monday.'

Children, seen here picking up hay, were expected to help on the land in the early 1900s, and they were allowed time off school if the weather threatened the harvest or the family was short-staffed

In those days the area was rich in wildlife and when Fred wended his way home through the dark woods his path was 'pin-pointed by myriads of glow-worms'. One day the schoolmaster asked the children to collect as many kinds of wild flower as they could on the first day of January, and Fred's friend Joan found an impressive sixty varieties. The birdlife was abundant too, and Fred loved to go bird's-nesting. For him that involved considerable risk, as much of his hunting ground was on the Hartland peninsula's 300ft cliffs.

That very exposed stretch of the North Devon coast has long been infamous as the haunt of smugglers and the graveyard of many a ship. But not all wrecks there were simply the result of storm and tempest. Fred's grandfather recalled sometimes being taken to the clifftop on a dark, stormy night, where a horse was being led to and fro with a lantern tied to its side. This was to entice a ship to come closer and founder on the rocks, so that the cargo could be plundered.

However, the local people were well known in the shipping world for their black deeds and were sometimes thwarted by alert captains. When a Greek ship ran aground in thick fog in 1922 Fred was among several people who rushed down to the shore to help. But they were confronted by a very wary captain, still on the bridge of his beleaguered vessel, revolver in hand and defying all.

That notorious coast also made the recovery of bodies very difficult and any not recovered within a day would be rendered unidentifiable by sharp rocks. So much so, there used to be a part of the local churchyard set aside for the burial of unknown sailors. Fred's generation knew it as 'Strangers Hill'.

Fred and his friends also used to scour the beaches after a violent storm, to see if anything useful could be found. But one day they had a real surprise, as Fred recalls:

'We were walking along at Hartland Quay when we saw what we thought was the body of a man washed up. But on looking more closely we saw that if was Jack Jeffrey, and we were relieved to see that this popular village man wasn't dead after all. Less than five feet tall and quite stout, Jack liked his pint of beer and he was obviously drunk. The reason for his condition was that he had gone down to the beach that morning and had found a small keg washed up by the tide. He had carried the keg to a spot above high-water mark and had opened it by making a small hole in the bung. Having discovered it contained brandy, Jack fixed the keg on a rock and lay on his back beneath it, allowing the precious liquid to drip into his mouth. When we found him his mouth was still open with the brandy dripping into it and out at the sides; it was surprising that he hadn't choked!

'We carried him up the steep cliff path to his home at Stoke – but getting so drunk didn't lessen his desire for alcohol. Several years later Jack worked for me on the farm, and he insisted on being paid every two weeks, so that he worked on a rota basis – two weeks on and one week off: during the latter he recovered after spending his two weeks' wages on drink. But he was a great character with whom to work, having a wonderful sense of humour and a kindly attitude towards everyone. It was a real sadness to all who knew Jack when he was eventually killed by a car while lying drunk in the road.'

There were other great characters in the village, too. 'Sam Cann said "Amen" at the end of each prayer in a very loud voice quite a while after everyone else, and it always seemed to me that the priest waited for him before beginning the next prayer. He was an old man when I was about to leave school, and as boys we loved to engage him in conversation. He was very fond of his pipe, so just as he was about to apply a match to the tobacco we would ask him a question which we knew would interest him. He became so engrossed in answering us that he continued to hold the lighted match until it burnt his fingers and he would throw it away in disgust. He then lit another, and another, with the same result, while we kepy plying our questions, and the pipe was not lit. I saw him use almost a whole box of matches during one conversation.

'Then there was Thomas Cory Burrow who, along with his two sisters, kept a paper shop for many years. He had a long beard and used to say that he had never shaved in his life. When asked why, he replied that his mother once told him that Jesus never shaved, so she felt he should not do so either.'

When Fred started school during World War I, labour was very scarce with men away at the front, so children were expected to help on the land as much as possible. The problem was exacerbated by the fact that many farmers had some of their horses commandeered by the army. Hay was taken away, too, and Fred recalls the very unsatisfactory system of the time.

'Sometimes a city-bred man would arrive at a farm without warning, saying that the authorities wanted this or that rick. He would then estimate the number of tons in the rick, into which he would put an iron bar with WD in large letters at one end, and a barb at the other to prevent the bar being removed before the hay was taken away by a War Department lorry.

'Some time in 1916 a cocky little character arrived at our farm demanding to be shown our ricks of hay. My father did as he was ordered, but then the official espied a rick which had not been pointed out to him; this was because it was of rushes, cut during the summer and used as winter bedding for cattle. To our astonishment he promptly stuck a WD bar into this rick also, and after measuring it announced that we should be paid for so many tons of hay. Naturally my father protested, saying that this rick did not contain anything fit for horses to eat, only rushes. But the little man simply made a joke of these protests, saying that my father should pull the other leg, too; and eventually a cheque arrived for so many tons of hay.

'Another example of waste that occurred on many farms during that war was that after a rick of hay had been commandeered and marked with the WD bar, it was often never claimed, even though the farmer had received his cheque. Those ricks remained, in some cases for three or four years, until the war ended and they were eventually used by the farmers.'

A good all-round countryman, Fred enjoyed traditional activities such as ferreting with nets. He also trapped moles and sold their skins for ninepence each, posting them off to Horace Friend, the dealer. But he was always close to animals and clearly recalls his feelings towards them.

'When the sheep were dipped each year the farmers would put the sheepdogs through the dip after the sheep – it was thought that any fleas would be destroyed in this way. But I did not like this practice at all and as a boy, just before the last sheep was put

through, I would slip quietly away with my dog Nun.

'Every animal kept on the farm served a useful purpose, and nothing was kept as a pet only. Even the cats were not allowed in the house because the purpose of having them was so they would destroy the rats and mice around the corn ricks and cattle sheds.

'When I was two a pony called Polly came to us and we grew up together. She was used a lot to pull Grandad's jingle, a small, covered trap in which he travelled about a lot because he had a heart condi-

tion. My brother and I often went with him and if we came to a hill us boys would often get out and walk. Also, Polly had learnt that when she was pulling Grandad uphill it was much easier to walk diagonally, repeatedly crossing from one side of the road to the other. She was a remarkable animal and it was one of the saddest days of my life when I had to have her put down, aged forty-two; it was as if we had lost a relative.

'Every animal on the farm used to be part of the family, and they almost knew you. Even when you got back home at 1.30am after Christmas Eve service you wouldn't

dream of going to bed without "having a last look", and feeding them a bit of cattle cake or something. And on the eve of Old Christmas Day (6 January) we gave the stock an extra meal, late in the evening after our final inspection.'

The Penningtons had worshipped at Stoke church since 1550 and Fred's family attended nearly every Sunday. Thus is was not surprising that, from a very early age, Fred had 'a wonderful sense of belonging to that lovely old building'. However, during his schooldays he was not consciously aware of receiving anything worthwhile from his religious education, so much so that when he reached the age of fifteen and went forward for confirmation, 'the whole thing seemed to be so meaningless' that he rejected the Christian faith completely.

In those days there was a very different attitude to church-going. 'Almost everyone went to church then, though perhaps not always for the right reason as there was still an element of Victorianism in our attitude to worship. But perhaps I am being too harsh in saying that, because I remember marvelling at the courage and devotion shown by so many farming folk in the face of great adversity and inconvenience in getting to church. For example, Dick and Lewis Avery hardly ever failed to be in their place each Sunday after walking some four miles from home in all weathers, despite Dick's deformed foot. Furthermore, they would have to be up and about early enough to tend the farm stock, before changing their clothes and setting off to walk to church and back again.

'There was a very real antagonism between the Anglican and Methodist churches in those days: no one would dream of going to a service in the other's church except for a funeral. I remember my grandfather warning me as a small boy never to go to the chapel because it was "of the Devil".

'However, everyone did get closer together from 11 November 1919, when the annual commemoration of the ending of World War I began. On the Sunday nearest to that date, all the ex-service men – about 120 in the years immediately following the war – headed by the village band some twenty-six strong, and with the schoolchildren bringing up the rear, marched to the parish church 1½ miles away for a remembrance service. In the evening we did the same at the Methodist church in the village, little thinking that we, the children, would be attending as adults twenty-six years later after another war – though then we would be remembering some of our own pals who had marched with us as children, and who had given their lives in World War II.

'Many people still believe that the churches were always full at every service in the old days, but Good Friday was certainly not well attended, at least not by the farming community. Practically every farmer set aside that day to dock his sheep, that is to trim the wool around the tail and hindquarters to prevent heavy soiling before shearing time arrived. If they were not docked at this time of year, blow-flies would lay their eggs in the wool, producing maggots which were a real menace in the days before there was effective veterinary treatment. Also, the man with a garden usually spent Good Friday making his first sowing of seeds and tilling his potatoes. But why these jobs were done on Good Friday I don't know. I can only assume the day coincided with the growth of fresh grass which made the sheep scour, and for most gardeners it was the first free day since Christmas.

'Another clear memory of Good Friday from my early days is of baker George Gifford coming round the farms very early, selling hot cross buns from his horse-drawn covered wagon.'

The Pennington farmhouse kitchen was typical of the day, dominated by a long, narrow table about 10ft by 3ft, with a bench of equal length on each side. Such seating capacity was essential at that time, especially on harvest and threshing days, when some fifteen men gathered for meals. During those busy times of year each man was given full board, which was considered to be part of his wages. And with free beer and cider his earnings came to about 25s a week. There was free milk and other perks, too.

Like most farmers of the day, the Penningtons were relatively self-sufficient, producing their own cream, butter and eggs. Excess butter was inscribed with the individual sign of the maker and usually sold in the pannier market at Bideford. Up to 20lb at a time had to be carried in huge baskets the one mile to the village, where it was put on a horse-drawn bus, later superseded by a motor bus. The carrier charge for each basket was 2d and the butter was sold for 4d a pound.

Along with the rows of home-made jams, pickles, chutneys and other preserves in the dairy were the 'steins', earthenware containers about 3ft high and 18in wide, in which eggs were pickled. In those days most hens were free-range and so laid predominantly in spring and summer; to overcome the lack of fresh eggs in winter, any surplus were kept in water-glass.

In those days it was traditional for the ladies of the household to look after both egg

A group of village women plucking turkeys en masse in preparation for Christmas – this was a hugely social occasion, always enlivened by gossip and singing, and the ribald telling of often lewd jokes and stories

and poultry production, rearing birds both for their own table and for sale. Many also reared geese, ducks and turkeys for the Christmas market. But turkey rearing was difficult, however, and fattening them could be cruel.

'Turkeys seemed to get every disease imaginable and to be ready to die at almost any moment. As children we were sent out to collect goose grass, known to us as "clider"; this was chopped very finely and mixed with the young turkeys' food, and was supposed to aid their delicate digestive systems. During the fattening period, some two months before Christmas, the turkeys were "crammed", when the food was physically pushed down each bird's throat every day until its crop was completely full; otherwise they would not eat enough to get them fat for the festive season.

'After the turkeys and other poultry had been plucked, the best feathers, especially those from the ducks and geese, were baked in the oven to sterilise them, and used to stuff pillows and mattresses.'

When Fred was just fourteen his parents sent him to Colchester Technical College, to develop his independence as well as improve his education. He went by rail, and even the journey was quite an ordeal for a young man who had never travelled at all.

Holsworthy market in 1909; the local livestock market, started in 1914, served a huge area, with dealers, butchers and farmers coming from as far away as Somerset to buy store animals; (opposite) A rest from haymaking. Fred is pictured back right

'It isn't easy for anyone nowadays to realise what a trauma it was for a lad of my age, who had never been further than twenty miles from home, to be suddenly thrust out into the unknown. It is also difficult for people these days to understand how limited a fourteen-year-old's knowledge of life could be at that time, in such an isolated part of the country. So little did we know of the outside world that I have heard men saying, when they came home after the 1914–18 war, that at the time they were called up they didn't know what it was all about.'

Another problem for young Fred was that he could not understand the Essex dialect, and equally his new friends found great difficulty in deciphering his strong Devon burr. But he persisted, and eventually settled in. However after eighteen months in Essex, he was subjected to another shock change: disaster struck the farm back in Devon, when on 19 July a severe storm devastated a half-mile strip of land across the Hartland peninsula. Several farms were ruined when huge hailstones destroyed all the crops grown as winter feed for the livestock. Many windows were smashed, too. The families could not afford to buy in extra feed so the livestock had to be sold before winter. As a result, Fred's parents were unable to meet the cost of keeping him at school, so at Christmas 1926 he returned to his home and former way of life. 'But now it was with a new vision of what it was all about.'

Despite his wider experience of life, Fred decided to pick up the threads of farming again. He was mostly influenced by his deep-rooted love of the land and animals, but also by the fact that the elder son was expected to continue the family tradition.

During the late 1920s the farming system still reflected the slow, limited nature of the transport system, as well as the closeness and insularity of the local community. 'A monthly livestock market was started in 1914, in a field adjoining the village. The auctioneers, Messrs Kivel & Sons of Holsworthy, held such markets in many villages in that area. There was no transport to take stock to a big central market, as is the practice today: cattle and sheep had to be walked up to four miles to the small markets dotted about the countryside, while pigs were taken there by horse and butt. Dealers and butchers from a wide area attended, as well as farmers from the better grazing lands of Somerset and other counties, to buy store cattle. All our pigs were sold as weaners – that is at 8 to 10 weeks old – and generally realised between 25s and 30s each. A two-year-old fat bullock would be sold for between £15 and £20, while a renewed, or freshly calved cow and her calf would fetch between £20 and £30. Fat lambs averaged about £2 each, while a breeding ewe would sell for £5.

'There were no pens for the cattle at the market: each farmer's stock had to be kept in a bunch beside the hedge, all around the field. Sometimes we had to stand there for up to four hours, often in wet weather, before our turn came to put the cattle through the sale ring.

'Hay harvest involved much harder work then, but it was always such an exciting time and almost always some friend from the village, or a neighbour whose hay was not ready on that particular day, would come at some time during the evening to lend a helping hand. There was no question of paying so much an hour – this was unheard of – because in the case of the neighbour we should be doing the same for him within a day or so. And the friend from the village was quite satisfied with his fill of cider from the stone jar kept in the shade of the hedge, and with the wonderful supper which was always provided when the day's work was finished.

'Swimming was a very popular pastime for many of us in summer. Many a time, after a long, hot day in the hay- or cornfield, we got on our bikes and dashed down to one of the little coves – usually Speke's Mill because it was the nearest – and plunged into the cool waters of the great ocean. Quite often it was dark before we left home, so we swam by moonlight.

'Speke's Mill was the scene of much activity in my young days, as Harry Balsdon supplied builders and farmers with sand from the beach. He used six donkeys with panniers to get it to the top of the cliff, from where it could be collected. Each donkey was loaded with about 2cwt of sand; it then staggered across the rocks and pools, up the steep, 200ft cliff path alone, and waited patiently beside a huge heap of sand until Harry came up with the last donkey: they were then unloaded. This continued until the tide came in. Then the donkeys were put in a field at the clifftop until the tide was right to start work the next day.

Hartland's Silver Star Dance Band in 1928, with Fred second from left

'We had some wonderful neighbours then, and they are so important in a farming community. Farmers depend a great deal upon one another for help of all kinds, from the loan of implements to help with transport. Also, each family would know exactly what was going on in the next home, and any variation in routine would immediately bring someone along to check that all was well. I remember once seeing a light shining in the kitchen of Leigh Farm, across the valley from my home, at three in the morning. We knew straightaway that something must be wrong, and on investigating discovered that our dear neighbour, William Pillman, had accidentally stepped over the bank of a stream and had drowned. That sort of occurrence brings people closer together everywhere.'

When Fred was about ten, his mother insisted that he learn to play the piano and he was taught by Miss Olive Taylor, whose father kept a draper's shop in the village. Later his tutor was Auriely Clay, whose father was the lighthouse keeper at Hartland Point. Every Saturday, Auriely cycled the four miles to the Pennington farm, up and down those steep hills in all kinds of weather. Two years later Fred was also given violin lessons by local postmaster Frank Christmas. At seventeen he was given organ lessons, and after two years he began playing for Hartland parochial church on a rota basis, when the old organist died.

Soon after he left school, Fred and four friends formed the Silver Star Dance Band. Dancing was very popular then, but organisers often had to bring in musicians from a long distance, or make do with a second-rate piano. Consequently there was plenty of work for a good new band, with the versatile Fred on saxophone and clarinet. The band enjoyed ten years' success, in the winter playing for an average of two or three nights each week throughout North Devon and Cornwall. Sometimes they attended dinner dances in 'big houses' – but for playing from 8pm to 1am received a meagre 5s plus travelling expenses. Fred also played drums and clarinet in the Hartland village band, of which he was master for many years.

Not only did the players enjoy themselves immensely, they also provided a valuable service for the local community. Fred admits that the quality of playing in both bands was not very high, although most local people thought it was superb. Fred attributes this to the fact that this was the first time many of the people had heard or seen *any* dance band, 'and anything must have seemed a great improvement on the out-of-tune piano or the wheezy accordion which had been their only means of accompaniment for as long as they could remember.'

The people also really appreciated carol singing. Apart from church services, it would be the only time they would hear Christmas music, and Fred remembers the fun they had. 'Some of the carols we sang must have been unique to Hartland, because I have never heard them sung anywhere else. The carol party usually started at The Anchor Inn, and we would black our faces with burnt cork, though I don't know why. Accompanied by an accordion player, or sometimes by two or three mandolins, the party set out to tour the parish, covering a part of it that night and the remainder on another evening, if they survived the first effort!'

During his teenage years, Fred finally decided to put the Christian faith on one side completely, and to look at what some other religions had to offer. He took every opportunity to study everything from Buddhism to Confucianism in his search for spiritual enlightenment, sometimes even reading about them while having his lunch beside the hedge when working in the fields.

Then Fred's mother started taking paying guests into their home, a development which had a great influence on him.

'It was almost as if I was meeting and talking to people from another world, just as I had done when at school in Essex. Some of our guests came year after year and became firm friends. Gradually many people came to our area for their holidays, and farmers welcomed the extra income during the agricultural depression of the 1920s. Before then you would never see a person who wasn't born and brought up here, except for delivery men and the odd trader. Then in 1921 the first "foreigner", a London stockbroker, decided to settle here, and after that the number of holidaymakers who retired here steadily increased. It was unfortunate in that the newcomers could pay more for the houses than our local lads could – but they did some good, too, in bringing new ideas to what had been a very introverted society.'

When Fred was sixteen he experienced a death in the family for the first time, when his grandfather died, aged sixty-seven after a heart attack. For Fred it was the end of an era.

'Funerals in those days almost amounted to feasts. There would be a three-course dinner for all who cared to come, after which the cortège set off for the church. Everyone walked, of course, and the coffin was carried by hand, in some instances for up to five miles. I have seen as many as a hundred men walking in pairs in front of a

coffin, and in front of them would walk the "time keeper": his job was to see that the leading four men stood out from the procession every minute, and waited, two on either side, until the coffin came abreast of them, when they took over the carrying until they reached the next four men.

'Deep black was worn at every funeral, the ladies being heavily veiled, while the men wore bowler hats; some of these hats looked a little tattered and green with age, since funerals were the only occasions on which they were worn. As the procession reached the church the "minute" bell would boom out from the tower. After the service my grandfather was laid to rest by six of his closest farming friends, in the part of the churchyard where his ancestors had been buried for over three hundred years. As was the custom, relatives, friends and neighbours went back to our home after the burial, where another feast was laid out. Then it was back to the normal work of the farm. Life had to go on: the cows had to be milked and the stock fed, no matter what else happened.'

In 1934 Fred married Dorothy, who was also from a farming family, and they lived in a little cottage attached to the Pennington farm. Through Bideford second-hand sales they were able to furnish their entire house for just £10, and with their new possessions plus their wedding presents they could set up a comfortable home.

A year later Fred's father decided to give up farming; he had never enjoyed good health, and he took on a hotel at Westward Ho! At the same time his brother went to work in London, so Fred was left to run the farm alone, with the help of employed

The village hall provided a suitable venue for all sorts of entertainment. This photograph shows an Old Tyme dancing class in progress

101

Scenes of Hartland village: (above) Lymebridge and (right) the Terrace

labour. But the hotel and farm were run as a joint enterprise, with the farm supplying eggs, butter, cream and so on.

So, after sixteen months of marriage, Fred and Dorothy moved into the farmhouse. But the beginning of their life together was overshadowed by enormous sadness.

'Our first baby was born, but due to a very difficult delivery she was injured at birth and lived for only one hour. Dorothy, too, was very ill for some time. Because the baby had died without being baptised, there was no burial service, so I gently wrapped her in cotton wool and placed her in a shoebox, which I strapped to the carrier of my bicycle, and rode to the churchyard where the sexton had prepared a little grave.'

Unfortunately for Fred, farming then entered a very difficult period. Furthermore, it became far less pleasant as the peace of ploughing with horses was replaced by the din of the tractor engine; and what had been a way of life became hard business. Fred began to wonder if God wanted him to do something else.

The Penningtons' two daughters were born in 1936 and 1937. Then in 1938 Fred's brother decided to come back into farming: however, the farm at Newton was incapable of supporting two families at that time, so the Penningtons decided to quit Newton and rent a larger farm at Holsworthy, where there was room for them all. Even though they only moved about ten miles, Fred was still very upset at leaving all the people and places he had come to love, not least the church.

When the war came, the Penningtons were ordered to plough up many acres of grassland, as were most farmers. Then the hotel was requisitioned by the military, so along with Fred's brother and his wife, Fred's parents took another farm on the same estate. But those war years were enriched by the arrival in Fred's household of two evacuee boys from the London slums and some prisoners of war who worked on the farm.

Also during the war, in 1942, an event happened which was to have a great influence on Fred's life in later years. He accidentally discovered that he could cure his young daughter's insomnia: not only could he put her into a deep sleep by stroking her forehead and saying 'You are going to sleep now Pam', but he could also rouse her simply by saying 'Pam, you are going to wake now,' two or three times. In other words, he discovered his ability to hypnotise.

Eventually, after years of heart-searching, Fred decided to become a priest, and as soon as he reached that decision he experienced a wonderful sense of peace. He and Dorothy went to live on his brother's farm, where he could work for him and earn enough to keep them while he studied for his general ordination examination through a six-year correspondence course. His final year's training was spent with the postgraduates of King's College, London, at St Boniface College, Warminster in Wiltshire. To complement Fred's course, Dorothy spent that year as a housekeeper to a priest in Devon.

Fred was the only man native to Hartland to have become a priest since 1474. He began his ministry as assistant curate to the rector of Tiverton, and when he and Dorothy moved in they were reduced to tears by the welcome. There were huge boxes

containing everything they might need for weeks to come, as well as charming letters of welcome from the parishioners. So they quickly settled in, and Dorothy shared the work of the Mothers' Union and the other parish organisations which a parson's wife is expected to lead. As an example of the goodwill with which they were received, Fred remembered that as Christmas approached, he just happened to mention to Reverend Worsley that he had no money to buy presents as his pay was so low; and then just a few days later he found an envelope containing £25 on his doormat, sent anonymously. Fred could hardly believe that such a sum was theirs and 'thanked God for the wonderful way in which he works'.

Not long after being ordained, Fred came to realise that he found his greatest satisfaction in ministering to the sick.

After three years at Tiverton, Fred took the living of Bradford and Thornbury, which was 'like going home again' because they were in the deanery of Holsworthy, where the Penningtons had lived for fourteen years. However, once again their enthusiasm was compromised through having to leave so many friends behind.

But Fred was glad to be back 'as in the old days', treading the soil that was so much a part of his nature. Indeed, he soon made good use of the land and sheds available and became deeply involved in the breeding of pigs, which he sold for fattening. He was to stay at Bradford and Thornbury for twelve years, but was always conscious of the fact that 'there is nothing that upsets a countryman more than for a priest, or anyone else for that matter, to come into a parish and start at once to turn everything upside down'.

Fred always liked the word 'parson' and encouraged people to use it. 'The term "parson" derives from the Latin *persona*, meaning "person", and I like to think of the parson as God's "person in the parish". The idea of the parish priest being called "Father" doesn't appeal to everyone, especially in the country parishes where he is known as "Parson So-and-So". It wasn't until I became a parish priest that I realised how close a parson and his people could be: he becomes involved not only in their intimate family and domestic problems and joys, but also in the wider secular and parochial organisations such as the parish council, school management and other committees in which he is expected to take a part. I believe it is right that he should be so involved because it helps to overcome the misunderstanding which some people have of seeing the Church only as a building, and a priest's work as being confined to that building. My experience has shown me that many opportunities occur in a secular gathering for Christian witness, because one is often then in the company of people who would rarely, if ever, be seen in church.

Fred and Dorothy with the first of their forty-five foster children

'This involvement on the part of the parish priest has the added effect of bringing him down from the pedestal on which people seem to put him – although at the same time one must keep a correct balance. The "hail fellow, well met" type of parson who goes round slapping everyone on the back is running the great risk of not being the priest or the teacher that he should be, but just "one of the boys". One has to learn the art of enfolding one's people in one's arms, metaphorically speaking, while at the same time gently keeping them at arm's length. I once knew a vicar who encouraged people to call him by his Christian name, children and adults alike; the eventual outcome of this policy, however, was that he had to leave his parish because he could not teach effectively any longer.'

After two years at Bradford and Thornbury, Dorothy and Fred felt that they were not being stretched to their full capacity. Only two of their nine bedrooms were being used, so they started to give holidays to deprived children. Then they began fostering children on a temporary basis, which would cover the whole year rather than just holiday times. Little did they think that they would foster no fewer than forty-five children in the years to come! In addition, this remarkable couple started to take in girls of fourteen to sixteen years of age who had become pregnant; they went on to help twenty-two of these unfortunate and often frightened people over the years.

Gradually Fred came to understand and develop his ability to help other people with deep mental problems, often through the laying-on of hands. In one instance a farmer who was not a dynamic Christian in any sense, and who only occasionally went to church, was so impressed by his wife's recovery that he decided to become a priest himself!

At this time Fred's concern became centred on a North Devon coroner's report, showing that the area had the highest number of suicides *per capita* of any area outside London. As a result, a branch of the Samaritans was formed and after a year Fred became its director. He found that most people who go to the Samaritans simply wish to talk, especially during the early hours of the morning when many find their loneliness to be most acute.

Eventually Fred was offered the living at Hartland, and his immediate reaction was, 'how wonderful'. But on reflection he felt that it would be unfair to the people he knew so well if he failed in his ministry because he was too familiar to them; and so he declined. Subsequently the bishop offered him North Molton with Twitchen, which he accepted, and later he took on Molland, too. In these parishes he found quite a different type of people from those in Bradford and Thornbury, and was, for instance, interested to note the different attitude to life taken by the farmers.

'The environment in which people are born and brought up has a lasting effect upon their spirituality. I found the farmers of Exmoor to be much more aware of the existence of God, and the reality of His love and power in their lives than was the case with their contemporaries in the more rewarding farming areas in other parts of the county. It seems to be a case of the easier life becomes, the less thought is given to the source of material things.

'For many years the farmers of Exmoor had scraped a living out of very reluctant and often harsh land, and the generation with which I was involved had been brought up under those conditions – always grateful for the little they had. But during my years on

Exmoor I saw a change take place. Largely because of the subsidies and grants given by the government, the farmers of Exmoor became more prosperous: many domestic luxuries and accessories appeared in their homes, for example, things that would have been undreamed of a few years earlier. Outside on the farms, too, the most modern equipment was being used, the cost of which must have been colossal. But with that change I noticed another and more insidious one, mainly in the next generation of farmers: a lessening of interest in things spiritual, and of the need to come to the source of all supply. Harvest festivals were still well patronised, but there seemed to be an underlying reluctance on the part of many to accept the fact that God alone supplies our every need. Yet in spite of that, it was among the farming community that I felt there was the deepest awareness of God.

Woolsery, where Fred and Dorothy lived in the 1970s

'In my visiting I came to know and love my people in their home environment; because of my farming background I was able to speak the language of the farmers and so enter into a close relationship with them. I was often able to help them with their milking, for instance, when they were ill, and in other emergencies on the farm. Because I had been in their situation I did not expect them to be in church at 8am when they had fifty cows to milk, or were in the middle of lambing four hundred ewes. But on the other hand, when they were consistently absent from church at other times, and made the excuse that they were too busy, I sometimes had to remind them that if there was a meet of the foxhounds or the staghounds in the village at 11am, they would find the time to be there.

'Twitchen is a beautiful little hamlet, higher up on the moor than North Molton, but nestling in a fold in the hills like its bigger neighbour. Here, as in most such isolated communities, there is a wonderful sense of comradeship. Everyone works happily with everyone else, whether it is in the skittles team, the Women's Institute or the church; barriers seem to be non-existent.'

Fred also grew to love the natural riches of Exmoor, especially the red deer 'which were very much part of the scene'. But sometimes nature worked against him, when snow and ice prevented him from getting across the moor to officiate at some services. With some of the hills having a gradient of one in four, he often became stranded and had to abandon the car after setting out for a service at one of the higher parishes.

As he became more involved in so many things, Fred gave up his Samaritans post after seven years; he wanted more time to devote to the parishes, and also to develop his interest in healing. Furthermore, for some years he had had an open mind as to the reality of a personal devil, since occasionally he encountered a situation which could not be explained away in ordinary human terms. He had become aware that 'Christ's Church is concerned not only with the healing of the body, mind and spirit as such, but also with that which often causes the sickness – the spiritual warfare against all forces of evil.' Therefore after much study and prayer, he decided that this would become part of his ministry. However, his first encounter with evil at an exorcism was very dramatic.

'My friend had been asked to visit a man whom it was suspected had been influenced by evil, and suggested that I should go with him. On arriving at the house we were shown into a room where a man was sitting in a chair with a dog at his side. Almost immediately he became very violent and abusive; his countenance became distorted, and he rose from his chair and rushed at my friend who calmly began to pray in Christ's name that he might be a channel for this sick man's healing, and that he himself might be surrounded by Christ's protecting power. By this time the man was in a terrible state of frenzy, and tried to grab my colleague by the throat; but for some reason which I didn't understand until later, he failed to reach him. My friend then began to command the evil power that was controlling this man to come out of him in Christ's name. This it did in no uncertain terms. The man then collapsed frothing at the mouth – a phenomenon that occurs at every exorcism, just as it did when our Lord cast out evil.'

After that, Fred was concerned about how he might react in such a situation on his own; so he started to prepare himself for the eventuality through prayer and meditation. Furthermore, there had recently been some unfortunate incidents in other parts of the country, in which much harm had been done by people who did not know what they were doing and were not even able to diagnose possession, let alone exorcise correctly. As a result, Fred's bishop, along with many others, decreed that no priest in his diocese should attempt an exorcism without first having referred the case to him. He also appointed four priests, including Fred, to supervise exorcism in his diocese.

Fred's most frightening experience of exorcism came when he was helping a nineteen-year-old man who felt a terrible urge to interfere with small boys, even though he knew it was wrong. After seeing Fred several times, during which he was hypnotised, the urge gradually lessened and then finally disappeared completely. However, about a year later the lad rang Fred. He was even more frightened and now had a new compulsion.

'For some time the horrible thought that he wanted to kill me came into his mind, especially as he sat at meals with a knife in his hand or looked at a blade in a shop window. Eventually it troubled him so much that his health began to suffer. He lost his appetite and couldn't sleep. And when he telephoned he was so shocked he could hardly share the secret with me. However, I persuaded him to come to my home.

'I realised that this was no ordinary case of mental disturbance, but that it might well be a very real devil possession; so I sought to prepare myself. I knew that I would be completely protected against anything that the force of evil could do to me, as I was surrounded by the love and power of Christ. At that moment this assurance took the form of a blue light enveloping me – something that I often experience while in meditation.

'When the lad arrived he was more relaxed than earlier, and I soon put him under hypnosis to diagnose his condition. I was rapidly convinced that the Devil had been thwarted in his attempt to destroy this lad when he tried to persuade him to interfere with small boys, and I had, as it were, come between him and his evil purpose. The logical conclusion seemed, therefore, that he might want to destroy me.

'As soon as the exorcism began, the lad's features became so distorted as to be barely recognisable as those of a human being. At the same time he rushed at me with a knife which he had pulled out from inside his sock. He came to within two feet of me, then suddenly fell back in his chair as if he had been pushed. At the third attempt he collapsed on the floor, again frothing at the mouth.

'I was anxious to hear from the lad why he had not been able to reach me with that knife so I made no attempt to heal the unconscious memory. After waking him I put that question to him and he replied: "There was a wall in front of you." My interpretation was that the spiritual protection Christ had afforded me became for the lad a physical wall which prevented him from harming me.'

Fortunately, Fred's ministry has involved no more than one or two cases of possession each year; but poltergeists have been much more common, and he has no doubt as to

their authenticity. In one case a lady was deeply distressed by the repeated movement of jewellery and clothing in her room when nobody had been there. When Fred was consulted, the first thing he did was to verify the claim; so he placed objects in the room, made a plan of where they were, locked the door and put the key in his pocket. When he returned to the room after an hour or so he found that the positions of the things had all been changed; indeed, some of them had been so arranged as to give the impression that someone was playing a game and laughing at them. But it wasn't difficult for Fred to displace the entity and bring peace to the troubled family. Through such work, Fred has come to be regarded as an important leader of the community. His personal charm has done much to allay fears of the unknown.

As well as bringing such great relief to the troubled mind, Fred has often triumphed over apparently incurable disease, not least cancer, which he believes is 'of the Devil'. In one case he not only saved a lady who was in the last stages of a carcinoma of the oesophagus, but also her son, who had been treated for a brain tumour.

In due course Fred and Dorothy started to take holidays at Hartland by courtesy of Sir Dennis Stucley, who owned the cottage in which they stayed. Each year they were delighted to spend two weeks at a spot which held so many happy memories; even the trees on which Fred had once carved his initials seemed hardly changed after nearly sixty years. One of their greatest joys was worshipping again in the church where they had shared so many wonderful experiences, especially with old friends.

Eventually Fred contemplated leaving his job as a parson in order to devote more time to his healing ministry. But he was not quite sixty-five, he would not get a full pension, nor would the church finance him as this was not official work. Therefore he put the decision on 'hold'.

Then Fred was offered the parsonage house at Woolsery, near Bideford, with the invitation to look after the parish of Hartland during an interregnum. Not only would this provide the space in which to help people, but also the opportunity to minister in the parish and church which had meant so much to him. However, Fred was constantly reminded that he was two generations apart from where he had been when he left Hartland. For example, one day when he went to visit a friend at home he was confronted by a familiar face, but it wasn't that of his old pal; neither was it that of his son – but his grandson! Furthermore, Hartland was now largely peopled by folk who would once have been classed as 'foreigners'.

After a year an appointment was made to the parish and Fred ceased to be priest-in-charge of Hartland. Then he was asked to take over the three parishes of Woolsery, Clovelly and Bucks Mills, which he did for two years. But this was to be the most unhappy period in his ministry, as he experienced the same problem of not being able to expand his healing ministry. It was not until 1980 that Fred was at last free to give his full time to the work he loved most.

After retiring from the ministry Fred described many of his remarkable experiences in a most enlightening book called *From Ploughboy to Priest*, published by Charles Herridge of Bideford in 1984. But his story was far from over. He is still consulted by some thirty people a week and deals with everything from drugs to anorexia nervosa, often accommodating patients in his own home in order to watch their eating habits. And patients are referred by doctors from all over Devon and Cornwall, as well as abroad. In addition he has sent hundreds of tapes to patients in places as far apart as Australia and America.

Now, he says, 'the old bird has finally come home to roost': indeed, he even lives in a house he knew as a child, when 'Sunset Cottage' was the home of a schoolfriend. Dorothy still supports him closely, and two of their foster children – now in their thirties – still live with them. And they remain surrounded by friends. Fred's only complaint is that they keep passing on and he has to take their funerals.

MUCH MORE THAN RUBBER STAMPS

ELIZABETH WILLIAMS AND JOY JOHNSON
Postmistresses of Shropshire and Oxfordshire

The village postmistress has often been caricatured as a shrivelled, embittered, grey-haired gossip, one who is quick with a rubber stamp but slow with help and advice. Yet generally, nothing could be further from the truth, as most postmistresses have been caring members of close-knit communities, serving very wide cross-sections of society. Two excellent ambassadors of the profession were Elizabeth Williams and Joy Johnson, both of whom set up sub-post offices in their homes during the 1940s and 1950s; they became closely involved in village life and were constantly helping others. For example, Elizabeth was a great friend to the illiterate gypsies who called in from time to time: not only did she read their letters to them, she also wrote their replies. 'Generally these notes were just enquiries after family health and news of new arrivals. The Romanies were always polite and very grateful for my help.'

If anything it was the postmistresses who were likely to be treated with disdain, rather than the customers, as Joy recalls:

'It was soon made clear to me that the regulars expected me to be a mind-reader, to know exactly what they wanted without being told. A stranger would stare in astonishment when a regular came in and without saying a word, put money down on the counter. Then I'd have to think . . . "Now that's Mr So-and-So and he wants a two-shilling postal order for his football pools and a stamp." And I'd hand them over with no word spoken except the customary "Good morning!" and his "Thank you, my duck," or whatever. There were many permutations of that, ranging from one lady just wanting a stamp for a monthly letter to Aunt Flo in Canada, to another pushing her family allowance book across the counter for me to date-stamp, tear out the counterfoil and hand over the 8s – all in silence!'

Neither Joy nor Elizabeth had particular ambitions to be postmistresses, but rather just drifted into it; in fact Elizabeth had wanted to be a teacher. One of three children, she was born on 27 March 1923, at Hinstock, near Market Drayton. Her father had been a coach-builder at Crewe Railway Works, but did not go back to this after the General Strike of 1926; instead he bought a 60-acre farm.

After school at Hinstock and Sambrook, Elizabeth won a scholarship to Newport (Shropshire) Girls' High School. On leaving, she kept house for a relative for some months, helped to nurse an invalid, and worked on the land before taking on the post office at the age of 25. Here she explains how this came about:

'The first post office that I can remember in Hinstock was started by a lady who had it until 1940. Then somebody else ran it with a shop but this got into difficulties, so I was able to start up in 1948. I was still living with my widowed mother at home, the eighteenth-century Homebrook House in the centre of the village, and it was there that

Homebrook House, Hinstock, where Elizabeth established a post office in 1948

The village postman was often a close friend
(courtesy of the Post Office)

we set up the post office, clearing the scullery and taking out the old sink, copper and bake-oven to make room for a counter and shelves.

'Hinstock had a population of about 600 and was a pleasant village with a war memorial on the village green, parish church, Methodist chapel, village school, two general stores, a sweet shop kept by an old lady mainly for the company of her customers, a veterinary surgeon (at first my grandfather, later my cousin), an undertaker and carpenter, two blacksmiths, a butcher who killed his own meat, and three pubs. My customers were nearly all connected with agriculture, being mostly farmers, farm workers, millers, milkmen and cattle hauliers.'

Unlike the postmaster before her, Elizabeth did not run a shop in conjunction with the post office; she did, however, sell some postcards and stationery, although there was not a great demand. Elizabeth's post office pay was only £22 a month, and out of that she had to pay for an assistant and provide a property. Her enterprise concentrated on basic post office business, as she explains:

'The post office was very important to the village for the sale of postage stamps (a letter then cost just 2½d, except for papers and unsealed envelopes which cost 1½d), for the parcel post, for postal orders, payment of pensions, savings stamps, saving certificates, and savings bank deposits and withdrawals. I sold a great many dog licences at 7s 6d and gun licences at £1, though very few game licences at £5. Road tax licences were not issued by post offices then. With the family allowance there was nothing for the first child, but 5s each for the others.

'I had to be up at 6.45am to receive the incoming mail, but once the letters had been sorted and the letter carriers had left, the office was closed until 9am; then it remained open until 6pm, except on Thursdays when it closed at 1pm. On Sundays I opened from 9am until 10.30am for the sending and receiving of telegrams.

'My mother helped in the post office, and my sister was a letter carrier, who once earned just 6s 6d a week, working two hours a day on six days. By 1946 her wage had risen to 22s a week. All four of my letter carriers were local people who did this part-time in conjunction with other work. In my time they all used bikes, but shortly before one went on foot. When one of the letter carriers retired I had difficulty in filling his place, so head office sent a man to do the round. When I discovered he did not know the area I sorted the mail for him and tied it into bundles, sending him off thinking that he could not get into too much difficulty. However, late in the afternoon someone came in for stamps and said that at lunchtime they had seen the man in a corner of a field with letters spread all around him. But next morning, when I asked him if he could cope, he assured me that he could.'

With customers ranging from eccentric to uneducated, Elizabeth often had reason to chuckle as she went about her business. Here she recalls a few of the more memorable villagers:

'The local squire was quite a character who had trained to become a priest but did not finish the course. Sometimes when the rector was on holiday he would take the church services, with much throwing around of arms and almost shouts. During the summer he used to walk around the village swinging a white horsehair fly-switch. He was held in little esteem and lived at the hall with his mother, while his wife lived at the neighbouring village hall.

'Then there was the old boy who used to be a road length'sman. He looked after a stretch between two convenient points, trimming the hedge banks, picking litter and so on, and was paid very little. But he was a very conscientious worker whose length was always clean and trim although he was almost bent double. He was a regular ringer of one of the church bells, and his philosophy was that there were just two things from which there was no escape: one was rent day, the other death.

'There was also a man who was mentally retarded, who always took his place to blow the church organ; even after we had electric put in for the bellows he would rush into

Over the years, many village post offices have been combined with shops. This picture was taken at Shipbourne in 1935 (courtesy of the Post Office)

church and sit in the back pew ready to man the pumps if necessary.

'But the funniest thing I remember was when an unmarried mother asked for a form to claim family allowance, then brought it back and asked me to check that it was properly filled in. Against "Name of father" she had written "No father"!'

Elizabeth was always closely involved in village activities. For example, she was on the committee to raise money to build a new village hall, she was also a member of the local church council, and she sang in the choir for twenty years. Today the church holds both happy and sad memories for her:

'One evening at a church meeting, the question was raised about what day in the year Jesus was born, and one lady was most upset when the rector said that the actual date was in fact not known, but that 25 December had been appointed because it fitted with the church calendar. Then on another evening, after the clocks had gone forwards, a lady came into church and walked up to the front pew as we were singing the final hymn, much to the amusement of the choirboys.

'On the Friday evening before Rogation Sunday, the church choir and congregation would make the traditional walk from the church. The route went past this piggery, and it was ironic that as we filed past it we were usually singing "Brothers, we are treading where the saints have trod"; there was usually quite a smell in the air, too! We then had a short sermon by the pool, finishing with a hymn at the war memorial.

'On 3 September 1939, when everyone was expecting war to be declared with Germany, our morning service began at 10.30am, so the rector's sister remained at home to hear the announcement at 11am. She then came to the church door and nodded to the rector with a pre-arranged signal, to say that war had indeed been declared. The rector then passed on the news to the congregation, and everyone knelt in prayer.'

During her time in the post office, Elizabeth was lucky in that she did not have any really awkward customers, although there were some who genuinely needed help; for example there was the lady whose hands were so crippled by arthritis that Elizabeth had to feel in her pockets for the money. However, Elizabeth herself was gossiped about from time to time – 'as were most people in the village; but it was mostly ignored, and soon passed.'

Crime was never a problem at Hinstock either, and the postmistress was never robbed or attacked. But in those days most villages had the benefit of a resident policeman. Elizabeth recalls the man at Hinstock:

'He was a good friend to many people and after a whist drive or dance would often walk my sister and I back home, especially if there were strangers about. One night after he had met his sergeant on point [a pre-determined meeting place], he was cycling home when he met a crowd of airmen on cycles, and none of them with lights. He turned off the road to let them go by, but they called him over to ask if they were going

Traditionally, the post office has been at the heart of village life,
as seen here at Hildenborough in 1936

115

the right way for their base. Unfortunately he had to tell them that they had already cycled six miles in the wrong direction! They had been to a dance at Newport, and when they came out they had seen some planes going over, and had followed their flightpath – the wrong way! So the bobby put them right, but asked them not to tell any other policeman that they'd seen him because he should have reported them for not having lights.'

Elizabeth gave up the post office in 1956, when she married and moved away. The business carried on in the same place for one year before the new postmistress moved it to a local shop. Today Hinstock has only one shop and one pub: the butcher, the baker, the undertaker and carpenter, the blacksmiths and veterinary surgeon have all gone. Elizabeth reflects sadly on the decline of village life.

'Most villages are now experiencing a great influx of people from towns, people who neither know nor wish to know about village life, nor to take part in local events. Their incursion is also making it very difficult for the young local people to find affordable homes, or even accommodation, so many end up moving away; this means there are few left who care about the closure of shops, churches and schools.

'In the old days everybody got involved with everything, and consideration for others and helping anyone in trouble made for a happy village. There was great community spirit when I was at Hinstock, which I suppose carried on from working together during the war; besides which the church and chapel congregations always co-operated for the good of the village.'

Today Elizabeth lives at West Felton, near Oswestry, and her husband has a 60-acre farm.

Although Joy Johnson was born in Birmingham on 6 February 1922, she spent all her school holidays on a Worcestershire farm: from her very first visit there she knew that her heart was in the countryside. Thus in 1947, as a young wife and mother, she seized the opportunity to move to a Cotswold village where she learned to enjoy a relatively primitive lifestyle. Her husband had contracted a serious form of recurring malaria while serving with the 1st Army in North Africa, and had been advised to live in the country after he was demobilised. So under the government's war agricultural training scheme the couple moved to Spelsbury in Oxfordshire, to a tied cottage 'like something out of Hansel and Gretel'. It was a big change for the daughter of the managing director of an engineering firm, one who had studied at King Edward VI Grammar School and was used to comfort! The new home had no electricity and no water on tap, and sanitation was a bucket privy down the garden. Water came from the village fountain, and all cooking and water-heating had to be done on the old black-leaded fireplace.

A year later Joy's husband took a farm job with a tied cottage in another part of Oxfordshire, and they moved away from Spelsbury. But in 1952 they heard that a church bungalow was for sale, and so took the opportunity to return to the place they loved. They had an acre of wilderness and worked a sixteen-hour day rearing hens, ducks and pigs as well as growing all their own produce. At the time, all the other houses in the village belonged to the owner of Spelsbury House.

But the 'good life' venture was not enough for the workaholic Joy, so when yet another unexpected opportunity arose, she welcomed it. She explains how fate took a hand:

'When we moved to Spelsbury the post office was run from the hallway of a cottage

The postmistress has always played an important part in the life of the village; her position enabled her to get to know everybody in the village community, though as party to a great deal of news-swapping and gossip she would have to exert her discretion and refuse to become involved should tempers run high!

and dealt basically with stamps, pensions and family allowances. But it served a most useful purpose as the nearest shops of any kind were in the market town of Charlbury, well over a mile away.

'In 1953 officials from Oxford head post office visited every cottage in Spelsbury trying to find a replacement for the retiring postmistress, then in her eighties. I was the only person prepared to consider it, so we had a lean-to built on to our kitchen.

'It was very much a sub-post office, dealing only in letters, parcels, stamps, pensions, postal orders, family allowances and national savings certificates. No licences of any kind nor post office savings books were handled. I had to requisition everything I required from head office at Oxford, when I submitted my weekly return of transactions.

'I had no other staff, but on the whole the work was very light and I had plenty of time to pursue my other activities with livestock and produce and so on. My hours of opening were 9am to 5pm on weekdays, and 9am to 1pm on Saturdays – until they persuaded me to sell newspapers on Sundays!'

Joy's parish included the hamlets of Ditchley, Taston, Dean and Fulwell, but Spelsbury was the recognised centre of activity as it boasted the church, the village hall, the school (later closed due to a lack of pupils) and the post office. The nearest pub was over half a mile away, the nearest policeman and doctors in Charlbury, and there were no shops of any kind in Spelsbury. The post office at Charlbury also acted as the area's telephone exchange, and the postmaster there connected all calls manually.

Inspecting the books: every few weeks an inspector from head office would descend on the village postmistress to check that everything was in order – not always with due warning, when he might be given a frosty reception! (Crown copyright)

The entire parish contained only a few hundred people, many of whom were related through inter-marriage, but until Joy became postmistress she did not realise just how broad a cross-section of humanity rubbed shoulders in this kind of cloistered community:

'We had the lady of the manor, the vicar and his wife, the schoolmistress, two farmers, the inevitable spinster sisters, a retired tea-planter and big-game hunter, employees of the manor farm, the elderly folk in the almshouses, and the occasional tramp begging for a cup of tea. There were also gypsies, some of whom tried to convince me that they were of true Romany blood and could tell my future; but most just tried to sell me odds and ends they had made.

'What fascinated me most was the village social structure, which seemed to have been set up by self-appointed "elders". Everyone was categorised according to a sort of "points" system depending on social background, education or wealth.'

Every few weeks an inspector would descend on Joy to check that all was running correctly; usually she was given warning of these visits, but on one occasion she was not, and the inspector in question was given a cool reception, as Joy relates:

'He said that he was from Oxford post office, and that he had arrived without warning to ensure that I had no time to prepare or to hide anything. Admittedly he produced an identity card, but I was not convinced. With outward calm I asked him to stand outside for a few minutes, which he did, and then I locked the door, rushed to the telephone

118

and checked his description with Oxford. When I was satisfied he was genuine I let him in, allowed him free access to my papers, apologised for my suspicion and gave him a cup of tea. To my relief he smiled kindly, saying that he'd made many surprise visits to post offices, but that this was the first time anyone had checked on him!

'One of these inspectors had been responsible for my several days' initial training in post office routine and duties, the most vital of which seemed to be remembering to change the date stamp before opening each morning. Until then I hadn't appreciated the power one can feel wielding a date stamp! I soon came to realise why people the world over fear or respect rubber stamps: just one thump of authority and your entire way of life can be changed! At the same time it was important that the rubber stamp's date was correct, to prove when something was posted.

'Having to sign the Official Secrets Act also gave me an inflated sense of importance for a while, but it was in fact an asset when I refused to involve myself in local gossip; for instance on family allowance or pension days the locals from the other four hamlets converged on my post office, and if it was raining or bitterly cold they would congregate inside to exchange news and gossip. Clearly they expected me to know all the local goings-on, and were very disappointed when they learned I was treating all information and activities as confidential.'

Another occasion on which Joy had a slight 'brush' with authority involved the police, as she explains:

'After helping to organise a large village fête at Spelsbury manor house I was asked to keep the takings – many hundreds of pounds and a positive fortune in those days – until the bank opened on Monday. But with so many people knowing about this, and because my premises were situated right on the edge of the village, I was rather apprehensive and decided we'd better take the cash to the nearest police station, at Chipping Norton, and ask them to keep it safely until Monday. They readily agreed, but it was such a large amount that, stupidly, I asked the desk sergeant if it would be safe there. With great patience he smiled, and said: "Madam, one hears of people trying to break *out* of a police station, but I've never heard of anyone trying to break *in*!"

'That was the only time I ever needed the police, as I was never threatened or frightened by anything. In those days you could safely leave the place unlocked when you were perhaps engrossed in work, right at the far end of the garden, and I could even leave the post office unlocked while I went to other rooms in the bungalow. Having to be anxious about security, as such, simply never occurred to anyone there, and most people didn't even bother to lock their doors at night.'

When food rationing ended in 1954, Joy was often asked by the locals if she would supply various items. As a result she had the post office enlarged to enable her to stock a small selection of food, toiletries, stationery, sweets and ice-cream. During the summer she started to provide ice-cream sodas, but came to regret this as there were so many glasses to wash. She also rued the day she agreed to make someone a few cakes, because her reputation for this soon spread, and she felt obliged to provide home-made cakes on a regular basis. Regulations concerning food hygiene were far less stringent then, and she was able to put out her produce in a glass display case specially made for the purpose. Christmas was a major challenge, as she was inundated with orders for cakes and mince pies; and in the summer there were large orders from Scout parties who camped in a nearby field. Everyone welcomed this new source of supplies as few people had cars and there was only one bus a day to the nearest market town.

Access to basic supplies was always a special problem during severe weather. Joy particularly remembers one bitter winter in the mid-1950s:

'For a few days we were totally cut off. Then a tractor somehow managed to break through to Charlbury and bring some basic necessities to us all. But with the telephone lines still down we continued to feel very isolated; when the postman finally managed to get through after six days he found the village postbox full of snow, ice and rotting mail! However, one of Charlbury's doctors captured everyone's imagination by using skis and snow-shoes to reach some of his patients. Most villagers were still dependent on the central fountain for their water, so they organised shifts to try to keep it from freezing completely. Even so, by the time some of them had staggered home with their buckets they found their water covered with thick ice which then had to be melted by the fire. When a lorry laden with supplies eventually got through there were loud cheers all round!'

When Joy first moved to Spelsbury she soon realised that the war had not touched the people there in the same way that she and other town dwellers had been affected. As she explains:

'This was largely because they hadn't known what it was to live through the blitzes or to queue endlessly for essential food. Although rationed to some extent, they had been able to have milk and eggs, and occasionally meat when a stock animal was slaughtered, as well as keep bees for honey; they also had the space to grow plenty of fruit and vegetables. Indeed, the only thing they really shared with townsfolk during the war was the separation from their loved ones, and the trauma sometimes of the tragic death of family members or friends.'

Among Joy's most unforgettable customers was the village 'Mrs Malaprop', who was a constant source of amusement and delight:

'She used to ask for items such as dislocated coconut and perforated milk, and once she announced that "The condescension on our windows is something awful". She also excitedly brought me the news of the local council's promise that the village was to be connected to mains water at last: "It was agreed anonymously," she said in triumph, "so they must all realise it was high time we had it." And then there was the time she commented on the Vatican's strange custom of sending up smoke signals whenever they "erected a new Pope".'

After six years Joy's circumstances changed dramatically and she had to give up the business. Fortunately, by then another villager was prepared to run the post office – though not the shop – from another cottage. A year later Joy moved to Oxford, as breadwinner to her two daughters. She now lives in Tring, and looks back with great affection on those Spelsbury days, 'when there was great community spirit and everybody shared and cared as though they were members of one big family'.

FROM HORSEBACK TO HELICOPTER

JOYCE DAMERELL

District Nurse and Midwife of Devon and Wiltshire

During some thirty years as a district nurse and midwife, Joyce Damerell used many forms of transport: she started with her 'own flat feet', progressed to 'a cycle thing with a motorised back wheel', then in 1948 she was given her first car, a Humber; but much more reliable for visiting people in remote areas were her horse, her pony and trap, and the helicopter which had to be called in during the prolonged snow of early 1963, when most of the expectant mothers were evacuated. But on one occasion in that record-breaking winter, when she was called out to Yelverton in a blizzard, Joyce had to walk to the neighbouring village of Crapstone to get a four-wheel-drive vehicle while the doctor made his own way on skis. Fortunately their mission was successful and together they managed to get their patient into hospital.

Joyce frequently had to abandon her car in severe weather and walk to isolated places on the moor. So whenever she changed her car she practised with the new model 'on long straights in the snow, to see how far it would slide. After all, it's no good discovering a weakness in a vehicle when you've got an emergency! Also, some of the roads were rougher in the old days, but at least that made them safer for horses.'

For most of her seventy-one years, Miss Joyce Damerell has enjoyed life at a cracking pace. Whether galloping across the moor to deliver a baby or follow the fox, nursing sick villagers or nurturing puppies, she has had a zest for life which has left most people at the stable door. For years in the hunting field the cry 'Nurse!' was as familiar as the huntsman's horn, and Joyce's first-aid training was often welcomed by those who fell by her side.

There were many occasions on her rural round when Joyce found herself in a tricky situation; once she was even threatened with a shotgun! As she went about delivering a baby, the over-anxious mother of the young woman giving birth repeatedly warned: 'You know what you can expect if you don't do a good job,' at the same time pointing to a gun standing in the corner. Joyce recalls that fortunately the grandmother was on hand to keep everything on an even keel, and 'at least it was a very good shotgun – a Purdey!'

A farmer's daughter, an only child and self-confessed tomboy, Joyce Rose Damerell was born at Plymouth on 27 September 1925. Her greatest influence was her grandfather, a builder, with whom she lived till the age of fourteen. 'He was a great Shot and a good dog handler, and very strict too. He liked quiet, and if he wanted to attract my attention he'd soon throw a clod of earth past my ear.'

When Joyce was at St Dunstan's Abbey School, Plymouth, she wanted to be a vet, 'but lady vets weren't thought much of in those days'. So at the age of eighteen she went

to the City Hospital Plymouth to become a state registered nurse. After her three-and-a-half years training she went to Paddington Hospital, London, where he sat her finals in midwifery.

Joyce was still only twenty-one when she had her first district, based at Overton, in Wiltshire. Her patch included half of Marlborough and went out to Silbury Hill. During the four years she was there the National Health Service was established (in 1948) and there was considerable conflict between the local health authority and the old nursing associations, who lost their power and for whom the district nurse used to collect a few coppers from the local people. Joyce recalls the tremendous waste of money when the NHS was instituted: 'Of course, when anything's free everybody goes for it, but with my training I helped to bring a new attitude. At first there was excessive use of dressings and many people were given false teeth and supports when they'd previously done without. But the Government soon brought in stricter control.'

The Wiltshire downs were ideal for developing an interest in horses, as Joyce recalls: 'It was a very good place for riding, up there on the Ridgeway. I got my Hunt button with the Tedworth. It was bestowed on me by the Master of Hounds, the Earl of Hardwick, and my greatest day was the first time I wore theHunt collar, which was green on a black coat. I hired a horse from Lady Jimmy Wright, the famous showjumper, for £5 a day, which was a lot to me as I only earned about £300 a year. I was very proud, but unfortunately many of the horses then were dreadful, with no "braking system". I was given an Appaloosa which wasn't castrated till it was eight and was still very bossy.

Then I bought my own horse from Oliver Dixon, the famous dealer at Chippenham, and an unkind ex-nursing association lady told me to get back into my station in life.

'Apart from sport, having a horse was a great advantage for generally getting about when petrol was restricted. It was quite something when rationing ended and I went to the garage and said: "Fill her up".'

At Overton, Joyce was also the village school nurse, and the first thing she noticed was how bad the children's deportment was. 'The area still suffered greatly through the old serfdom system, with much tugging of forelocks, and no one paid any attention to the children.' To help rectify this, Joyce, who had many awards for competitive dancing, started to teach ballet to four girls in her drawing room. Almost overnight the class increased to about twenty, including pupils from the neighbouring village of Lockeridge, so the group had to move to the village hall.

On leaving Overton, Joyce took a post as a senior midwifery sister at Flete, the home of Lord Mildmay; he had offered the house as a maternity home for expectant Plymouth mothers away from the stress of the air raids on the town. As a result of this work, Joyce realised her calling was to district nursing and enrolled for a six-month course to become a Queen's nursing sister.

Joyce's first appointment, in 1953, was to the pretty village of Buckland Monachorum, between Tavistock and Plymouth. Her patch stretched from Postbridge and Dartmeet, in the middle of Dartmoor, to Clearbrook and Buckland Monachorum itself. She lived in a tied cottage which she later bought, and this is still her home. Apart from her work, a lifelong interest has been fieldsports; in particular the training of gundogs, at which Joyce has been extremely successful. A person with whom Joyce shared these interests was an ex-vicar of Buckland Monachorum, whom Joyce recalls with great affection.

'He was Christopher Hughes, the parson before this one; he was also a sporting vicar and we got on famously as he established a shoot here. When he discovered my interest he said: "Ah, pointers! Well, they'll need something to point at!" and he showed me two or three hundred pheasants coming on nicely in his garden. As in other villages he also held the charity money with which I could buy prams, blankets and other things for anyone deserving. I generally bought the prams very cheaply at the local auction house, but there was little demand for them and they sometimes gave them to us. The charity money resulted from bequests but amounted to very little. One, for bread, was for only 10s a year, but had been a substantial sum when instituted centuries ago. In those days we had some really poor people whom we used to cook for. I recommended the deserving people – mostly elderly folk or those out of work – to the Mothers' Union. There was no meals on wheels then.'

In addition to poverty, Joyce recalls some very primitive and insanitary conditions in her district, both in Wiltshire and on Dartmoor.

'Like most other fairly unspoilt areas, we had some genuine Romanies but they were always fascinating, and – through my work – some became great friends, bringing me horses to look at and giving me tea to drink. But we always went in twos to visit one family because you needed someone to keep granny under control while you did your work. She always wanted to be present at the birth of anyone in her family, but although their caravans were perfect, her hands were always dirty. The men were always sent outside, and they sat around a "witch's cauldron" boiling water for me; though before I could use it I had to skim the top off.

'But whatever the conditions, you always had to be careful not to offend people by refusing their hospitality. Generally I never had an alcoholic drink, except on Christmas Day when I was careful to start with a good, greasy breakfast to line the tummy! First stop would be at a certain old lady's by the river, where I'd be given blackberry wine. Then it was over to the old major for half a tumbler of gin, then on to someone else for port, or whatever. "Go on, it's good for you nurse," they'd say, and it was hard to resist. But what you couldn't do was take from one and refuse another, because they'd soon find out!

'Even so, there was one offer I had no hesitation in refusing. When I was at a squatters' camp on Marlborough Common this tramp asked me in for breakfast and made me look in the pot which he had hanging over an open fire. There was this chicken, not only unplucked but also undrawn! He told me he'd found it dead on the roadside.

'The camp had been a hospital during the war but was eagerly adopted by the homeless when it was abandoned. There was a great shortage of housing then and anywhere dry and warm was soon taken up. The camp people were on my patch and I had to look after them the same as anyone else.

'Also in Wiltshire, I used to visit this family who lived in the middle of a wood and were very poor. One day the mother's stew was just bacon bones and cabbage, with all this fat floating on the top. Poor woman, she could never get her words right. Once, when I was giving her a choice of immunisation dates she said: "Nurse, it's all *invenereal* to me". Another time, when I caught her on the hock and she was flustered, she said: "Nurse, I'm *prostitute*".

Lambs' tails were a favourite Devon dish early this century, often cooked in the open field*

'Immunisation was quite an old thing, and at the mother-and-baby clinics we'd always given cod liver oil, concentrated orange juice and dried milk to combat deficiencies.

'Fleas were a common problem. One day when I went to turn the mattress of a 22-stone lady who'd been discharged from hospital after fracturing her hip, I was smothered with them; when I went home I had to take a bath with all my clothes on. So I approached the lady and told her about the old trick of using a wet bar of soap to catch them. But she was a sweet old soul and said: "Nurse, don't 'e worry: every time I feels a bugger bite I catches 'im!" I was told that fleas didn't jump as high as Wellington boots, but that didn't help and in the end I infected my own house, as every time I returned home a few fleas would abandon ship before I reached the bathroom! There was very little help from the health authority in the control of fleas so all I could do then was suggest changing talc for DDT! Luckily, most people were very clean and would talk openly about their problems. It was always best to say: "What are *we* going to do about it?" Then you had a partner rather than an enemy.

'Conditions were generally at their worst during the war, when I had scabies, impetigo and head lice repeatedly, even though you were supposed to wear a snood to keep your hair in.'

Joyce has long respected the moor people who have often had to endure very tough lives, and she has vivid memories of their fortitude.

'Over the years I've been here they've had to go out and feed their stock in some atrocious weather, and when I was out visiting it was quite a common occurrence to see one of the wives battling against a blizzard with a ewe across her shoulders, a sheep she'd

---

*After scalding, the wool was pulled off, the tails soaked in salted water overnight, dried, rolled on a warm surface to remove any remaining wool, washed again, cut up, boiled until nearly tender, and cooked in a pie with chopped onion and seasoning

dug out of the snow. But they can be cussed folk. Once I was called to the heart of the moor, but I lost my way in the dark and had to ask for directions at this remote farmhouse – and these people came to the door with a poker. A lot of moor folk had no electricity in the early days, but when it was laid on and television came in they became much more aware of a wider world. Also, better lighting helped me in my work.'

Inevitably, people who led very insular lives were particularly prone to superstition, although most of their beliefs, such as never take May blossom indoors, were harmless. However, taken to extremes by simple-minded folk, some of the old convictions led to tragedy, even as late as the 1970s. Sadly, one or two of Joyce's stories are so gruesome they must remain untold to protect the living relatives of victims.

By way of contrast, Joyce has also witnessed the good effects which strong beliefs can achieve. 'Dr Willington, an ex-general practitioner here, taught me about hypnosis, and together we trained expectant mothers in self-hypnosis; some were so successful they had no discomfort at all with their births. It's a shame that hypnosis has been so popularised on TV, because this has trivialised it and people are now afraid of making fools of themselves. Yet it's one of the best tools available. But a nurse can only use it with a doctor's permission, and they aren't all so keen.

'I've also seen animals helped with less conventional methods. One of the old healers, Mr German, was very good and did a lot with cattle, stopping bleeding and curing many ailments; I've even seen infections mysteriously disappear.

'With the introduction of the NHS the biggest change in maternity care was that the midwife could send for the doctor without asking the mother's position. This made us feel more in control. Previously mothers had resisted calling in the doctor because they had to pay. Admittedly many doctors did not charge those who couldn't afford it, but there was always a certain amount of pride involved.

'Also in 1948 we were given maternity boxes with sterilised pads and suchlike. Since then there has been such a change in outlook. Whereas we used to have to persuade mothers to go into hospital, with all the equipment on hand, now it is rare to have a baby at home.'

When Joyce arrived at Buckland Monachorum, the care of the dead was quite different from today's routine. Here she describes the procedure followed in those days:

'When I first came here it was customary for the nurse *not* to lay people out too often as this task provided a little income for a local lady who was treated with great respect in the community. And once or twice when I did it the local people were surprised when I forgot to open the windows: they believed this stopped the soul going out to leave the body in peace. Also, in the old days if you laid out a person you were off midwifery for forty-eight hours because of the bugs. So altogether you tried not to do it. Nowadays the undertakers lay people out after you've notified the death.'

In a rural district, with relatively few people on hand to help, the ability to cope with accidents and emergencies was essential to Joyce's job, not least in midwifery. Quite a few of the hundreds of babies which she delivered on her own arrived in this world in very awkward places, including cars. Once Joyce thought she would have to deliver a baby on a mattress on the floor because the family concerned could not afford a bed, but 'something went wrong' and the mother was admitted before she actually delivered.

A nurse on an ABC scooter, a studio portrait taken in 1929. This was a popular and highly fashionable mode of transport at the time

For some years now it has been the practice to admit to hospital all diagnosed cases of twins or other multiple births prior to delivery, but until recently 'forecasts' of such events were far less reliable. On one occasion Joyce was there 'just in time to catch the first of twins' and when the doctor arrived he said to her: 'I think you know more about it than me!'

When I asked Joyce if Christmas deliveries were special she replied: 'They may be to the mothers, but only a bit to the nurse because everybody's special and you're privileged to be there on the arrival of their baby. Also, you can't help thinking of the Christmas dinner you've left at home! Even now, after I've been retired twenty years, I get local people stopping me to say: "Don't you know what today is?" "No," I reply. Then they say something like, "Twenty-eight years ago today you delivered my son," as if they expect me to remember everything. But basically, as a district nurse you were a servant to the people, and you nursed a family right through.'

At one time Joyce's kitchen was the waiting room to her surgery, and the facilities were used by the first chiropody clinic run by the Red Cross. Joyce's clinics were mainly attended by children coming home from school with cuts and bruises, as well as messages. Indeed, generations must have grown up with the idea that she was always there when needed. One of the best compliments she was paid was when a lad came to the door and said: 'Will you come now as Mother's very ill.' Without hesitation, Joyce picked up her bag and went to assist. But when she arrived at the boy's house his mother was furious because she had only had a headache and had lain down on the sofa to rest! The resourceful lad had taken it upon himself to summon nurse Damerell.

Quite a few of Joyce's patients – and sometimes their relatives – had to be handled with considerable tact. Joyce remembers some of the more awkward ones:

'This old chap came to the door and his feet were in a very bad way. His nails were so overgrown he'd cut holes in his shoes to let them through, so he asked me to cut them. I said: "OK, but you must soak them in soda first." This was duly done and I went back on another day to do the dressing. But when I asked the wife if she would like me to bathe her husband while I was there she screamed blue murder: "You hussy you, taking advantage of my husband; clear off!"

'Sometimes the elderly gentlemen were quite flirtatious, even in their eighties. If they were alone a lot up in their bedrooms, and you went to do things such as blanket baths, they could get a little bit wild. Some old chaps would actually say: "I'm being a naughty boy, aren't I nurse?" yet they'd still carry on. But you had to treat every patient as an individual. Some of the ninety-year-olds were very self-possessed, and you had to be a little bit careful as they were looked on with esteem!

'In the old days a lot of people were very wary – they didn't talk much to the outside world, and you had to treat them with sensitivity and consideration. You couldn't just breeze in and lay down the law. It was generally much better to bide your time and,

The local health visitor weighing a newborn baby, delivered at home, in the early 1960s

131

perhaps while admiring their bullocks, casually offer to return the following day to give gran a wash and brush-up, or whatever.'

Over four decades Joyce has seen many changes in and around Buckland Monachorum. Here she describes some of the most important:

'There has been a considerable rise in the population, yet there has been a fall in the number of shops, from three grocers, a wool shop and a separate post office to just one which incorporates the post office. However, we have managed to keep our one excellent pub, The Drake Manor. There used to be a great many Nissen huts which were used for housing, but the council moved the people out onto new estates. Since then, commuters have moved in to many of the better houses, but they have really supported the village well, and taken it over to good effect.

During the severe winter of 1962–3 the helicopter was an important lifeline for isolated rural communities
(Western Morning News)

'The hall was originally built by the WI and run by them only, with two meetings a month, but as time went by interest diminished. Now the building has a billiard hall attached; it is known as the village hall, and is mostly run by the commuters. Groups such as the Brownies, Guides, Scouts and youth club are all important to village spirit, too.

'I used to be a governor of the old local school, which has now been converted into two nice dwellings. The new school is only twenty years old and is well made, it takes children up to eleven and has good teachers. Also, we are lucky that it is a church school, with the vicar's frequent contact.

'We used to have tremendous village flower shows, with the longest beans and all that, but the gardens are not the same now and people don't have the time to grow so much. But we still get good flowers and cakes displayed.

'Once there were lots of hares and partridges hereabouts, but I wouldn't know where to find even one now, and there are only a few grouse left on the high moor. The Dartmoor National Park is trying to stop us working dogs up there, but what we do is very important as we are asked by the great moors in the north of England and Scotland to help with pre-shooting season grouse counts. There was a time when I was an adviser to the national park, but not now. Overall, the decline in songbirds and flowers has not been particularly significant round here, but the red tape has increased tremendously.

There's a special orchid on the moor and nobody is allowed to pick it – but when you talk to the old people they say they used to gather it by the bunch every year, yet plenty always remained.

'I used to be on the parochial church council, and I regard a good church as the centre of a rural village. When I came here we had a Baptist chapel as well as the COE church, St Andrews, which now shares a vicar with Milton Combe. All the enthusiastic Baptists of former times have died, but the chapel remains as a Baptist hostel and hall used for general village activities.

'St Andrews is now well supported by all ages and has become something of a music centre. We have a very good group there, with instruments such as guitar, piano, flute and oboe, and some people come to church just to hear them or our excellent choir. It's all much more relaxed in church now, with less formal dress; in the old days, if two people attended with the same hat there'd be panic!

'The only real controversy at church now is over this new concept of christening. In the past I've christened sick babies which looked poorly, with no questions asked – that has always been accepted practice for nurses; then the children were christened properly afterwards. But nowadays it has all become much too complicated, with godparents obliged to attend pre-christening talks and to watch videos to make sure they know what their commitment is. This is turning many people away from church, when all should be accepted without question. It's later, with confirmation, that all the serious stuff can be addressed.'

Overall, Joyce regards Buckland Monachorum as 'a lovely, balanced village, with lots of history; a place where I can go to church, put my hand on that end pew and think of all the previous generations which have been there.' Out in the streets she enjoys speaking to everybody, and always gets a wave when people pass. But then, she did deliver many of them.

Sadly, Joyce died in early 1997 and did not live to see this book printed. However, part of the text was read out at her funeral, as a tribute to her extraordinary life.

LEADER OF THE COMMUNITY

JOHN FAIRLESS

Schoolmaster of Ayrshire and Peeblesshire

As the 'dominie' (head teacher) of a rural school in Scotland, John Fairless was highly regarded in the village community and, along with the parish minister, expected to play a leading part in local activities. He was therefore not only teacher at two tiny Borders schools but also, at various times, the district registrar, presiding officer at the polling station, chairman of election meetings, village librarian, organiser of evening classes, a church elder and treasurer, JP, committee member of the local horticultural society, and the organiser of village sports, clubs and functions.

An only child and the son of a bank teller and clerk, John Aitken Fairless was born in the small country town of Beith, Ayrshire, on 5 November 1926. His earliest memory is of having his tonsils out at the age of four, in the living room at home – a common practice then – while seated on the knee of his mother's help. Later, during the early years of World War II, he had to sleep on a camp bed in the living room because two evacuees from Glasgow occupied his bedroom. And when Clydebank was bombed he spent the night under the living-room table. Much more pleasant are memories of helping out in nearby hayfields.

Most of John's schooling was at Speir's School, Beith; Speir's was then fee-paying, and its preparatory department was like a rural school with only two teachers, one taking primary grades 1–4, the other grades 5–7. John thrived at Speir's, playing both rugby and cricket for the school and becoming the school captain, and in due course he was to be very grateful for the good example set by teachers there. However, he spent the last few months of his sixth year at Peebles High School, the family having had to move to Peebles because of his father's ill health.

John did not have any particular ambitions while at school, and when he left in 1944 he started work as an archivist clerk at the Foreign Office in London. In January 1945 he was called up and joined the Intelligence Corps, in 1946–7 serving in Malaya, where he was interviewed and accepted for emergency teacher training. After taking an MA degree at Edinburgh University and then following a teacher training course at Moray House College, Edinburgh, he opted for primary teaching. He applied to Peeblesshire County Council and in 1952 was appointed to Kingsland Primary School, Peebles, to take a primary 6 class.

In 1953 he married Pam; ten years later he was appointed dominie at Stobo, a very small village a few miles west of Peebles, and so became closely involved in country life. Here he was the only full-time teacher and, with never more than fifteen pupils, taught all the stages of primary 1–7.

Harrow farm cottages at Stobo. The local workforce was mostly employed in forestry and farming on the large estates of Stobo and Dawyck, in beautiful countryside in the Tweed valley

Station Road, the main street of Eddleston, in the early 1900s.
John and his wife moved to Eddleston in 1971, when closure of Stobo school seemed inevitable and
John took up a new teaching post at Eddleston school

John was immediately impressed by the beauty of Stobo's surroundings in the valley of the River Tweed. Most of the local people were employed in farming and forestry on the large estates of Stobo (on whose land the school was built) and Dawyck, and he and Pam were to spend eight very happy years there. The children were polite and respectful and John would very rarely need to use the tawse (leather strap).

Stobo's first school, held in the substantially Norman kirk, was set up after the Reformation of 1560, as in other parts of Scotland. Grooves still visible in the stonework of the church porch are thought to have been made by pupils sharpening pieces of slate into pencils called 'skaillie'.

The village's first separate school was erected in about 1640, after a new law decreed that a school should be built in every parish. In about 1777 a schoolhouse was built for the schoolmaster and his family; it was extended and modernised in 1914, and was the origin of the schoolhouse which John took over. It was attached to the replacement school built in 1887, largely to accommodate more pupils, the parish population having risen from 338 in 1801 to 467 in 1881. In 1792 there had been only twenty-four pupils, but the new school was built to accommodate seventy, at a cost of £300. While building work proceeded, lessons were again held in Stobo kirk.

Stobo's first schoolmasters should have been paid by the parish heritors (landholders obliged to contribute to the upkeep of the church), but the latter managed to avoid this until 1745. Then they agreed to pay the schoolmaster a guaranteed salary of 100 merks (old Scots marks of 13s 4d each), equivalent to £5 11s 1¹⁄₃d per year, a sum supplemented by fees paid by pupils and by the master taking on jobs such as church beadle (the officer attending the minister) and precentor (the leader of singing), later session clerk and keeper of parish records. It is also said that the master increased his income through organising cockfights for his pupils, not only charging the children to watch but also keeping the defeated cockerel for his own use!

In 1834, examples of annual fees paid by pupils at Stobo were: English 4s 6d, English and writing 6s, arithmetic and English 7s 6d and Latin 12s. At that time, the owner of Stobo estate paid the fees if a family had more than two children at the school.

In the 1940s, when John Fairless was studying, most teachers were still relatively poorly paid, earning only about £15 a month ('less than a bus conductress'). As dominie, however, John did receive annual perquisities from the Stobo estate: namely a load of manure for the garden, a brace of pheasants at Christmas and a fishing permit for the local stretch of the River Tweed.

A typical 1930s classroom, all very regimented and orderly

Before publicly managed school boards were established in 1872, the Scottish educational system was supervised by the Church of Scotland presbyteries; these aimed to provide the majority of the population with basic skills in 'the three Rs' by way of establishing a school in each parish. Although few pupils from areas such as Stobo went on to burgh school or university, the system worked well in the countryside and resulted in a higher percentage of the population, including many of the poorer people, acquiring basic skills than was the case in England. Indeed, records show that in 1834 there was no one in Stobo parish over the age of fifteen who could not read and write.

Under the 1872 Act, education became compulsory for children aged 5–13. Supervised by the Scottish education department, each school board, elected every three years, kept a register of all the children in the parish, and it could prosecute any parents not sending them to school regularly. Each board's minutes provide a fascinating record of the times: for example, from Stobo's 1873 minutes we learn that the teacher's salary was fixed at £50 'with all the fees and Government allowances'; plans for school water closets were discussed; and children were charged a shilling each for coals for the season. In 1880 they recorded that all rat-holes were to be filled up, and in 1883 that a shelter shed where children could wait in wet weather was to be provided at an estimated cost of £12.

John Fairless was only the sixth schoolmaster at Stobo since 1879. Like the others, he and his wife were obliged to live in the schoolhouse next to the school, rent and rates being deducted from his salary at source.

For most of the twentieth century the average number of pupils at Stobo was about twenty, some travelling from as far afield as Stobohopehead, a remote shepherd's cottage involving a daily round trip of some nine miles on foot. Numbers temporarily increased when nearby schools at Lyne and Drumelzier were closed. Although children from outlying districts eventually had the benefit of bus and car transport, heavy snowfall sometimes prevented them from attending school. Temporary closure was also caused by a hurricane in 1969, when fallen trees blocked the roads.

During John's time at Stobo the parish population was less than half what it was when the new school was built in 1887, and since then it has decreased even further, many farm cottages having been sold and owners commuting to Edinburgh. As a result class numbers were very small, and Stobo children had the benefit of very close attention from the teachers; it is therefore not surprising that John had no problems with truancy. Here he recalls lessons in the 1960s:

'The curriculum was quite broad, the subjects taught including reading, writing, spelling, English, arithmetic (later primary maths), history, geography, nature study (later environmental studies) and religious education. When primary school French was introduced I gave my senior pupils a simple course using illustrated pamphlets and gramophone records. We also had visiting teachers each week for art, music, physical

Schoolchildren at their Christmas party in the 1950s

139

education (very cramped when inside the school) and needlework. Guest speakers included a former water bailiff who spoke about the life of the salmon.

'Religious instruction was given every day, usually first thing in the morning. After the Lord's Prayer we listened to the religious service for schools on Radio Scotland; the local minister conducted a service in the school most Wednesdays, and hymn singing was popular. At Christmas the children performed a Nativity play in the local church.'

John formed the school's first parent-teacher association, to help raise funds to purchase items such as extra reading materials, as well as to encourage parental interest. PTA events included beetle drives, sales of work and school concerts.

There was an excellent community spirit in Stobo, as John recalls:

'Everyone gave their full support to all village activities, particularly to school functions. For example, the community Christmas party which I instituted in the village hall was a great success and attended by all ages, from babes in arms to grandparents. The ladies provided a sumptuous buffet, the gentlemen paying half-a-crown and the children free. After the meal there were games and dances.

'School Christmas parties were held in the village hall and were paid for by the Countess of Dysart, the owner of Stobo estate; she provided presents for the children, too. She also paid for their annual summer outings, which included a visit to the David Livingstone memorial at Blantyre, and a sail down the Clyde on the paddle-steamer Waverley.

'Stobo was a lovely place to live in, with most kind and friendly people who were very helpful to me. The school was just like a large family where the older members looked after the younger ones. School was much less complicated than it is now, both for teachers and pupils.'

Of course not all events went smoothly, and sometimes they resulted in considerable humour, as John recalls:

'At the school concert in the village hall the infants were doing a Red Indian number when one of the boys' head-dresses slipped down over his eyes, causing great amusement among the audience. On the second night the little boy wanted to go on stage again with the head-dress over his eyes because, as he said to a helper, "a gie'd them a guid laugh!" [I gave them a good laugh.]'

There were some great characters among the villagers, too. John particularly recalls Miss May Anderson, the postmistress and shopkeeper:

'She was one of the kindest and most helpful people you are ever likely to meet. When the doctor was known to be in the area it was the custom for May to place a large Union Jack in the hedge, hanging over the road, outside the post office. On seeing the flag, the doctor, who was perhaps then on his way home, would call in to learn of other visits he had to make. This saved him from being called out from Peebles again.

'May used to operate the manual telephone exchange at the post office, night and day, and because every call went through her she was in touch with the whole community. If she learned that anyone was in trouble she would go out of her way to help. Once someone missed the local bus at the post office so May phoned me to stop the bus, and the passenger was brought by car while the bus waited at the school.

'May also held a regular chiropody night in her house, and she often fed the sales reps who called at her shop.'

Mrs Fairless was herself a fully qualified infant teacher, and taught at Kingsland Primary School in Peebles for a number of years. She was also closely involved with the children at Stobo, largely because the house adjoined the school; thus as well as helping at school functions, she tended to most of the children's cuts and bruises.

The schoolhouse was situated right beside the road, its prominent position often bringing various other requests for help, many of which Pamela remembers well:

'Coming from Peebles, ours was the first house for quite a few miles, so we had to deal with callers of all descriptions in various states of distress, day and night. Running out of petrol was common, as were breakdowns, and it was often a farmer. Once John had to get up in the night to take someone home as we never kept petrol in a can.

'Another time, when we were in bed on a really frosty night with Jack Frost paintings on the windows, there was a ring on the doorbell. But by the time we had "come to" and got up and scratched a clear bit on the window to see out, there was no one there. Later we heard that the caller had a leaky radiator and had sought help at the post office, but the postmistress had been afraid to open her door and had directed the people to the cottage at the other end of the row, where the gamekeeper lived. He had put a coat on top of his pyjamas and come out with a jug of water, but unfortunately his door had slammed and locked him out!

'Sometimes people called just because of a wasp sting, and hikers and campers frequently got into difficulties. They would see Stobo on the map and decide to walk there to have lunch, only to find that there was no inn or hotel; so they often finished up sitting at our kitchen table.

'One day three girls on a Duke of Edinburgh Award hike got lost while looking for the youth hostel and started to walk along the Tweed while it was in spate. They came to a burn which was also heavy with water, and decided to jump across. One did so successfully, and then her kit bag was thrown to her, but unfortunately this fell back into the water and was swept down into the Tweed. Stupidly the girl tried to save it, and she too ended up in the Tweed. Luckily the others managed to grab her and pull her out, but the bag sailed off. They appeared at our door just after this, their faces white as sheets; they had been thinking they were going to have to spend the night in the phone box when they had seen our light. After making pools of water on our kitchen floor, they got dried and changed and we gave them a meal and a bed for the night. The joke was that their anoraks hanging up to dry were covered with place-name badges proclaiming that they'd been all over Europe – and they had to come to Stobo to get lost!

'Several weeks later the girls phoned to say that the kit bag had been pulled out of the Tweed at Kelso, over fifty miles away, with only two items missing from the top!

'Stobo schoolhouse was a great place for tramps. I used to think that somewhere on our wall there was some sort of a sign – maybe a stone on top of another – to say "This is a good place!" We never gave them money but *always* something to eat. I never felt afraid or threatened, even if I was on my own in the house. I used to tell the tramps to sit on the garden seat at the front and I'd bring them food. Our "watch-dog" usually sat at their feet. Sometimes I was handed an old syrup tin for the tea, but when filled these were decidedly too hot to handle so I had to serve them on a tray, or fix on a wire handle.

The village was flooded when Eddleston Water broke its banks

One day I was handed a simply filthy Thermos flask – the tramp was none too clean, either – and I decided to scrub it until it was shining both inside and out. I thought I'd maybe start the man on the road to cleanliness!

'At that time a huge dam was being constructed for Edinburgh's water supply and many men looking for work passed our door on their way there. I expect they slept in the hedges and begged for food all the way. They often had sore feet, so to cool and wash them I would send them to the burn with a bit of old towel and a clean pair of socks. All the people in the cottages were of the same inclination, never refusing food, and sometimes we discovered that we had all had a visit, thus giving the tramps a supply in their pockets for any inhospitable place they came to.

'All the time we were there we were never broken into to or had anything taken. But it was interesting to note that if a stranger walked up the railway line, for instance, everyone knew at what time he had passed their house and could give a good description of him.'

At the schoolhouse, Mrs Fairless also had to accommodate student teachers who came for two weeks at a time and expected a quiet life. But they soon learned that a rural headteacher's job was certainly not a 9–4 one: the dominie served and led the whole community, with the constant help of his wife.

When there was an election, Pamela was expected to supply lunch and tea plus umpteen teas and coffees to the returning officer (John), his clerk and the duty police-man sent from Peebles. Furthermore, as all the people came down to vote they took the opportunity to call on Pamela, and so she generally ended up serving beverages in the schoolhouse all day.

Electioneering meetings, however, were generally far less popular in this traditionally conservative area. Indeed on one occasion when the SNP candidate came to the school nobody at all turned up except for the two organisers – John and the minister, Dr James Bullock, who was to have chaired the meeting. But that was not the end of the candidate's embarrassment because when he went to leave, his motorbike (plus sidecar) – covered with home-made political slogans – refused to start until John and James gave a push. The disillusioned candidate disappeared into the darkness, having forgotton to switch on his lights; although in the circumstances it was perhaps just as well that he left so discreetly!

Fortunately, frequent entertaining was something that Pamela enjoyed, and there was no problem with supplies as Stobo was well served by vans from shops in Peebles or one-man businesses. These included a fruiterer, a baker, a butcher and a walk-in grocer's van, and some called twice a week, becoming good friends over the years. When the weather was cold they too came in for yet more coffee!

John and Pamela also had visits from previous residents at the schoolhouse, and these were always pleased to discover that – in those days at least – little had changed. One 80-year-old gentleman, a retired doctor called Jervis, was the son of the man who had been Stobo dominie from 1879 to 1914. Then there was Daisy Glover, whose father had been dominie from 1914 to 1933; she, too, had become an infant teacher, at nearby Innerleithen. When she lived at Stobo she and her sister went by train to secondary school in Peebles every day, a trip which once a week Daisy turned to particular advantage, as Pamela explains:

'The railway line passed Stobo schoolhouse as it ran down to the little station near the smithy and post office. On Tuesdays it was always fish for tea, which Daisy had bought in Peebles – someone from the schoolhouse would stand in the field beside the line, and as the train passed Daisy would throw the parcel of fish out to them. By the time she and her sister had left the train and walked home down the road, the fish would be frying merrily on the stove.'

As the number of children continued to decline, the closure of Stobo school seemed inevitable; in 1971 John therefore reluctantly took a post as head of two teachers at Eddleston Primary School, a few miles to the north. However, he played a leading part in persuading the authorities to rescind the decision to close Stobo school, a public meeting voicing strong objection on the grounds that the school was a vital focus of community life. Subsequently, improvements to the building were made and an extension completed in 1976; but later, the number of pupils was projected to fall below ten and the Borders Regional Council finally decided to close the school in 1983. Existing pupils were given the choice of transferring to Peebles or Broughton schools, and today Stobo children are provided with transport to Broughton, some five miles away. Ironically the potential school roll at Stobo grew after the decision to close. However, the building continued to be used for community purposes, at first housing the village shop and post office as part of Stobo Countryside Centre and later a workshop.

At Eddleston, John and Pamela were again obliged to occupy the schoolhouse, although this time it was not attached to the school. Here John taught primary 4–7 while his lady assistant taught 1–3, to a roll of 30–40 pupils. Most lived in the village and were brought in by bus.

At first the school curriculum at Eddleston was much the same as at Stobo, but before John retired in 1985 marked changes had taken place. Decimalisation was introduced in 1971, more projects were undertaken and teaching methods generally became less formal, a trend already prevalent in many rural schools. Today John feels that there is too much informality in teaching and that children generally have suffered through lack of discipline. He still believes that 'a disciplined child is a happy child'.

As at Stobo, John became a leader of the community at Eddleston. For example, as head teacher he inherited the job as chairman of the children's entertainment committee, which each year held a Christmas party, a fancy dress parade and a summer sports day. Traditionally the dominie was also secretary of the local horticultural society, so each year John had to organise the flower show. He became the first chairman of Eddleston Community Council, he was a church elder, and for a time the session clerk.

Here, too, the pupils provided John with many amusing memories, such as the time when he had just finished reading out the Queen's special Commonwealth Day message. One of the infants, a farmer's son, remarked to his friend: 'That was real nice of the Queen to write to us.'

Although John and Pam were very happy in the community at Eddleston, John found that teaching there was not quite as rewarding as it had been at Stobo. This was partly due to changes in educational methods: there was more administrative work, much of which had to be done after the children had gone home, along with the correction of school work. But the main reason was that both Eddleston and the school were considerably larger, the village population then being about 400–500; as a result it was not such a close-knit community, particularly as many more people worked outside the village. As John said, 'It was no longer just like a family.' Even so, 'dominie' Fairless served his new village well, and now, from his retirement home in Peebles, he can look back with great pride on his time as leader of two country communities.

Keeping Order in Church

On the 17th April 1725, John Rudge bequeathed to the parish of Trysull, in Staffordshire, twenty shillings a year, that a poor man might be employed to go about the church during sermon and keep the people awake; also to keep dogs out of church. A bequest by Richard Dovey, of Farmcote, dated in 1659, had in view the payment of eight shillings annually to a poor man, for the performance of the same duties in the church of Claverley, Shropshire. In some parishes, persons were regularly appointed to whip dogs out of church; and dog-whipping is a charge in some sextons' accounts to the present day.

In the parishes of Chislet, Kent, and Peterborough, Herefordshire, there are similar provisions for the exclusion of dogs from church, and at Wolverhampton there is one of five shillings for keeping boys quiet in time of service.

At Acton church, in Cheshire, about five and twenty years ago, one of the churchwardens or the apparitor used to go round the church during service, with a long wand in his hand; and if any of the congregation were asleep, they were instantly awoke by a tap on the head. At Dunchurch, a similar custom existed: a person bearing a stout wand, shaped like a hay fork at the end, stepped stealthily up and down the nave and aisle, and, whenever he saw an individual asleep, he touched him so effectually that the spell was broken; this being sometimes done by fitting the fork to the nape of the neck. We read of the beadle in another church, going round the edifice during service, carrying a long staff, at one end of which was a fox's brush, and at the other a knob; with the former he gently tickled the faces of the female sleepers, while on the heads of their male compeers he bestowed with the knob a sensible rap.

The May-pole

Not content with a garlanding of their brows, of their doors and windows, the merry people of the old days had in every town, or considerable district of a town, and in every village, a fixed pole, as high as the mast of a vessel of a hundred tons, on which each May morning they suspended wreaths of flowers, and round which they danced in rings pretty nearly the whole day. The May-pole, as it was called, had its place equally with the parish church or the parish stocks; or, if anywhere one was wanting, the people selected a suitable tree, fashioned it, brought it in triumphantly, and erected it in the proper place, there from year to year to remain. The Puritans – those most respectable people, always so unpleasantly shown as the enemies of mirth and good humour – caused May-poles

RAISING OF THE MAY-POLE.

to be uprooted, and a stop put to all their jollities; but after the Restoration they were everywhere re-erected, and the appropriate rites recommenced. Now, alas! in the course of mere gradual change of manners, the May-pole has again vanished. They must now be pretty old people who remember ever seeing one.

Beating the Bounds

The Gange Days are the same as the three Rogation Days (the Monday, Tuesday and Wednesday before Holy Thursday, or Ascension Day), and were so called from the ancient custom of perambulating the boundaries of the parish on those days, the name being derived from the Saxon word *gangen*, to go. In Roman Catholic times, this perambulation was a matter of great ceremony, attended with feastings and various superstitious practices. Banners, which the parish was bound to provide, hand-bells, and lights enlivened the procession. At one place the perambulators would stop to feast; and at another assemble round a cross to be edified with some godly admonition, or the legend of some saint or martyr, and so complete the circuit of the parish. When processions were forbidden, the useful part of these perambulations was retained. By the injunctions of Queen Elizabeth it was required that, in order to retain the perambulation of the circuits of parishes, the people should once in the year, at the time accustomed, with the curate and substantial men of the parish, walk about the parishes, as they were accustomed, and at their return to the church make their common prayers. And the curate in these perambulations was at certain convenient places to admonish the people to give thanks to God, as they beheld his benefits, and for the increase and abundance of the fruits upon the face of the earth. The 104th psalm was appointed to be said on these occasions.

The writer recollects one of these perambulations in his earlier days. The vicar of the parish was there; so were the 'substantial men', and a goodly number of juveniles too; but the admonitions and the psalm were certainly not. It was a merry two days' ramble through all sorts of odd places. At one time we entered a house by the door, and left it by a window on the opposite side; at another, men threw off their clothes to cross a canal at a certain point; then we climbed high walls, dived through the thickest part of a wood, and left everywhere in our track the conspicuous capitals R.P. Buns and beer were served out to those who were lucky enough, or strong enough, to get them.

The ancient custom of perambulating parishes in Rogation Week had a two-fold object. It was designed to supplicate the Divine blessing on the fruits of the earth; and to preserve in all classes of the community a correct knowledge of, and due respect for, the bounds of parochial and individual property.

The custom of perambulating parishes continued in some parts of the kingdom to a late period, but the religious portion of it was generally, if not universally, omitted. The custom has, however, of late years been revived in its integrity in many parishes, and certainly such a perambulation among the bounties of creation affords a Christian minister a most favourable opportunity for awakening in his parishioners a due sense of gratitude.

PARISH STOCKS.

Parish Punishment

Three centuries ago the flagellation of vagrants was carried out to a cruel extent. Whipping, however, was not always executed at the 'cart's tail'. It was, indeed, so ordered in the statute of Henry VIII; but by that passed in the 39th of Elizabeth it was not required, and about this time (1596), whipping posts came into use. On May 5th, 1713, the corporation of Doncaster ordered 'a whipping post to be set up at the stocks at Butcher Cross, for punishing vagrants and sturdy beggars'. The stocks were often so constructed as to serve both for stocks and whipping-post. The posts which supported the stocks being made sufficiently high, were furnished near the top with iron clasps to fasten round the wrists of the offendor, and hold him securely during the infliction of the punishment. Sometimes a single post was made to serve both purposes; claps being provided near the top for the wrists, when used as a whipping-post, and similar claps below for the ankles when used as stocks, in which case the culprit sat on a bench behind the post, so that his legs when fastened to the post were in a horizontal position. Stocks and whipping-posts of this description still exist in many places. Latterly, under the influence, we may suppose, of growing humanity, the whipping part of the apparatus was dispensed with, and the stocks left alone.

All extracts taken from *The Book of Days*, 1866 by R. Chambers

The stocks was a simple arrangement for exposing a culprit on a bench, confined by having his ankles laid fast in holes under a movable board. Each parish had one, usually close to the churchyard, but sometimes in more solitary places. Now-a-days, the stocks are in most places removed as an unpopular object; or we see little more than a stump of them left. The whipping of female vagrants was expressly forbidden by statute of 1791.

Bleeding Horses

A curious superstition was formerly prevalent regarding St Stephen's Day – that horses should then, after being first well galloped, be copiously let blood, to insure them against disease in the course of the following year.

Superstitions about Diseases

One sometimes sees people with a clumsy-looking silver ring which has a piece of copper set into the inside, and this, though in constant contact throughout, is supposed (aided by the moisture of the hand) to keep up a gentle, but continual galvanic current, and so to alleviate or remove rheumatism.

This notion has an air of science about it which may perhaps redeem it from the character of mere superstition; but the following case can put in no such claim. When I was a boy a person came to my father (a clergyman), and asked him for a 'sacramental shilling', i.e., one out of the alms collected at the Holy Communion, to be made into a ring, and worn as a cure for epilepsy. He naturally declined to give one for 'superstitious uses', and no doubt was thought very cruel by the unfortunate applicant.

Ague is a disease about which various strange notions are prevalent. One is that it cannot be cured by a regular doctor – it is out of their reach altogether and can only be touched by some old woman's nostrum. It is frequently treated with spiders and cobwebs. These, indeed, are said to contain arsenic; and, if so, there may be a touch of truth in the treatment. Fright is also looked upon as cure for ague.

Equally strange are some of the notions about smallpox. Fried mice are relied on as a specific for it, and I am afraid that it is considered necessary that they are fried alive.

With respect to whooping-cough, it is believed that if you ask a person riding a piebald horse what to do for it, his recommendation will be successful if attended to. My grandfather at one time always used to ride a piebald horse, and he has frequently been stopped by people asking for a cure for whooping-cough. His invariable answer was, 'Patience and water-gruel'; perhaps, upon the whole, the best advice that could be given.

Earrings are considered to be a cure for sore eyes, and perhaps they may be useful so long as the ear is sore, the ring acting as a mild seton; but their efficacy is believed in even after the ear has healed.

Warts are another thing expected to be cured by charms. A gentleman well known to me states that, when he was a boy, the landlady of an inn where he happened to be took compassion on his warty hands, and undertook to cure them by rubbing them with bacon. It was necessary, however, that the bacon should be *stolen*; so the good lady took it secretly from her own larder, which was supposed to answer the condition sufficiently. If I recollect rightly, the warts remained as bad as ever, which was perhaps due to the bacon not having been *bona fide* stolen.

Hidden Priests

During the 150 years following the Reformation, Catholicism was generally treated by the law with great severity, insomuch that a trafficking priest found in England was liable to capital punishment for merely performing the rites of his religion. Nevertheless, even in the most rigorous times, there was always a number of priests concealed in the houses of the Catholic nobility and gentry, daring anything for the sake of what they thought their duty. The country-houses of the wealthy Catholics were in many instances provided with secret chambers, in which the priests lived concealed probably from all but the lord and lady of the mansion, and at the utmost one or two confidential domestics. It is to be presumed that a priest was rarely a permanent tenant of the Patmos provided for him, because usually these concealed apartments were so straitened and inconvenient that not even religious enthusiasm could reconcile any one long to occupy them. At Watcombe, in Berks, there is an old manor-house, in which the priest's chamber is accessible by lifting the board on a staircase. Others were hidden behind a stack of chimneys, accessible only by removing the floorboards. Some had back staircases concealed in the walls; others had places of retreat in their chimneys; some had trap-doors, descending into hidden recesses.

Turnspit Dogs

A few months ago the writer happened to be at an auction of what are technically termed fixtures; in this instance, the last movable furnishings of an ancient country-house, about to be pulled down to make way for a railway station. Amongst the many lots arranged for sale, was a large, wooden wheel enclosed in a kind of circular box, which gave rise to many speculations respecting the use it had been put to. At last, an old man, the blacksmith of the neighbouring village, made his appearance, and solved the puzzle, by stating that it was a 'dog-wheel', a machine used to turn a spit by the labour of a dog; a very common practice down to a not distant period, though now scarcely within the memory of living men. Mr Jesse, the well-known writer on rural

to be seized upon to perform it. If the poor animal, wearied with having a larger joint than usual to turn, stopped for a moment, the voice of the cook might be heard rating him in no very gentle terms. When we consider that a large joint of beef would take at least three hours before it was properly roasted, we may form some idea of the task a dog had to perform. If he stops a moment to rest his weary limbs he is then kicked about the kitchen when the task is over.

In 1800, at an inn at Newcastle, a pleasant village near Carmarthen, great care was taken to ensure

subjects, recalls, in his youth, watching a turnspit in operation at the house of a worthy old Welsh clergyman in Worcestershire: 'He taught me to read. He was a good man, wore a bushy wig, black worsted stockings, and large plated buckles on his shoes. As he had several boarders as well as day scholars, his two turnspits had plenty to do. They were long-bodied, crook-legged, and ugly dogs, with a suspicious, unhappy look about them, as if they were weary of the task they had to do, and expected every moment

that the turnspit dog did not observe the cook approach the larder; if he did, he immediately hid himself for the remainder of the day, and the guest had to be contented with more humble fare than intended. One dog being insufficient to do all the roasting for a large establishment, two or more were kept, working alternately; and each animal well knowing and noting its regular turn of duty, great difficulty was experienced in compelling it to work out of the regular system of rotation.

All extracts taken from *The Book of Days*, 1866 by R. Chambers

LIVING OFF THE FAT

VICTOR WILSON
Butcher of Staffordshire

For much of his long life Victor Wilson has literally lived off the fat of the land because in the old days, when he butchered local livestock, scarcely any part of an animal was wasted, including the fat. Victor recalls those days of 'waste not, want not':

'Everybody used to eat a lot of fat meat in themma [those] days; in fact they used to say that it had to be fat to be good. There were always a lot of spare fat left over when the meat was trimmed, and one of the first things I had to do, when I started in the shop as a boy, was sort out the "first and second fat". There were a good demand for both in themma days. The good stuff went for food, the dirty for tallow, which was used for making candles and soap, and for greasing machinery.

'The people who picked up the fat also took the cow hides, which made as much as £2 to £3 each before the war, but the price for leather has never been so good since plastic took over.

'We also sold sheepskins and all the animal bones. Another thing the skin lorry took most of was our tripe. As a lad one of my jobs was to open up the tripes, shake all the muck out, wash them well and then hang them up to dry. It was the sale of all these by-products as well as meat which made the difference in earning a reasonable living.'

Such practices seemed entirely natural to young Victor George Wilson because his family had been butchers at Abbots Bromley, Staffordshire, at least since the 1851 national population census. Victor was born on 16 August 1922, at the Bagot Street shop and house which his parents had moved into only a few months before. Prior to that, his father and grandfather had owned other shops in the village. Today Victor clearly remembers his early years, with his three sisters, in one of Abbots Bromley's many half-timbered, typically Staffordshire buildings, dating from before the sixteenth century:

'From the shop you went straight into the living room, and Dad would often leave his supper and go through to serve, as we were open to 9.30pm every day. And when we were closed people would often come to the back door, even on Sunday, when all the family always went to church. But, of course, in the country you knew all these people.

'I went to the local school from the age of five until I was ten, and then to the school at Uttoxeter from age eleven to fourteen. When I started to help in the shop my parents gave me a shilling a week to buy a national savings stamp from the teacher.

'The roads had tarmac then but there were no kerb stones, and, anyway, there were only about a dozen cars about. I went out delivering meat on my bike every day in Bromley, cycling to three kitchens five mornings a week before 8am! We sold most of

The Wilsons' shop is a typical half-timbered Staffordshire building, dating from before the sixteenth century

the meat in this village, in Newton, Admaston, Bromley Hurst and in Hoar Cross. Regular customers in Abbots Bromley included the vicar and doctor, but I only ever saw the maids. I went twice a week to the boys' home at Hoar Cross, and daily just down the road to the private school of St Mary's and St Anne's, though not Sunday, and not Friday which was fish day. Another butcher served the school at the same time. The local baker supplied their bread, and farmer Cotterell sold them milk and potatoes; so they always consumed a lot of local produce.

'The post came twice a day, by bike in the morning and by van from Rugeley in the afternoon. Our family's first car was a Ford, and we got a local garage to cut the top off and put a van top on. We bought it in about 1936, a year or so before we bought our first 'frigeration unit.

'Electricity came here in the mid-1930s, before mains water. There were about four public wells and pumps around the village, but even so there was a bit of queuing on wash mornings. We had our own well, and to us the water was perfect – until the water company came along and said it were no good! We got running water in about 1936, the year I left school.

An evacuee drawing water from the cottage well during World War II

'When I was at school I didn't have any special ambition. You didn't have much choice really. Everybody 'ud tell you you had to stop home and help your Dad. It's cheap labour too!'

When Victor started working for his father at the age of fourteen he was paid 'about ten bob a week'. In those days there was another butcher in the village and competition was strong. Here Victor describes some of the favourite meats, and the common butchery practices of the 1930s:

'In the shop we had just a wooden counter and a window board to lay the meat on. When meat was delivered by trap it was simply laid on a sheet on the wooden floor of the vehicle. Like most people, we were very fond of boiled brisket for breakfast, first pickled in water with saltpetre and salt, which came in big blocks. This was also popular because there were no fridges then. Also, the sausages were made without preservatives and had to be eaten within a couple of days, so we always made them on a Friday night for the big Saturday trade. It wasn't worth making them all the time. In any case, there wasn't a lot of pork

Victor and his father in 1928 aboard the trap used for meat deliveries.
Note their slogan: 'Tender meat, the dentist's enemy'

about then, so there wasn't the meat to make many sausages. We made only pork sausages and they sold for between 10d and 1s 3d a pound. Today the rules say that a sausage must contain at least 65 per cent meat – but you want at least 75 per cent for a good banger!

'Best beef wasn't above about 1s 3d a pound, and steak 18d to 2s. Beef liver was always very popular and you could get about 12lb from one animal. There was only a little game about and it was more expensive then. Lord Bagot had the only gamekeeper in the area. There weren't many turkeys, either, as they were difficult to rear then: a farmer would often lose twenty out of fifty birds, so they were a luxury in themma days. Also, we didn't do well on chickens as so many farmers sold their own – it was their wives' Christmas money.

'Dad would buy animals on the hoof mostly once a week, usually from Rugeley or Uttoxeter markets, or from local farmers who came in and said they had a good beast for sale. He had a horse and cart – a proper cow cart – as well as a trap, and he'd collect pigs and sheep. The same trap in which meat was delivered was also used to go to nearby market towns, when stabling was often provided at inns. But very local cattle were usually walked in, sometimes by us. Singles don't come very well and cattle are much easier to handle in twos, so I often ended up chasing them across the fields. Some animals were bought from the cattle market which was held here at Abbots Bromley twice a year, but the cattle lorries killed that off.

'We always did our own slaughtering. With a cow you had to get your rope over one horn and under the jaw; not around the neck, else you'd strangle it. The rope were passed through a ring in the wall and the animal pulled into position, with its head over a block. Then father pole-axed the cow bang in the middle of the forehead, so that it was stunned, and then he'd slit its throat. If you were lucky you could get two or three gallons of blood, and my job was to catch it.

'We used the blood to make a bit of black pudding. Ideally, as well as the blood you

153

Slaughtering pigs was a messy affair

want pork leaf fat, groats, leeks or onions, and seasoning. As soon as the blood is cold you mix everything in, then you put a skin on the end of a funnel and fill it up. The best skins come from a cow gut, but you can use pig's. After that you loop the filled skins up to get the rings, then put them in the boiler for about thirty minutes. A lump of soda in the water would help to turn the pudding black. It usually kept for about a week and you could see when it was going off because it grew whiskers on the outside.

'I was only about eight or nine when I first went out pig killing with Dad. There were no fridges then, so this always had to be done in frosty weather. It was always a time-consuming process and the farmer would have to make an appointment. He would also need to have about twenty or thirty gallons of boiling water ready for us.

'Pig killing wasn't always straightforward because a sow can be funny with a stranger. Dad would loop a rope in the pig's mouth and then around its leg, and then the farmer helped him to get the animal on its side. But you had to watch it all the time as the pig might suddenly get up. They often didn't bother to stun the pig, just slit it. It was often cruel in themma days. After the pig was bled and gutted, boiling water was poured all over it to soften the bristles, which were scraped off head to tail – it was easier in that direction. Then you rolled 'im over to do the other side. Next you hooked it up, in the kitchen, dairy or cooling house, because it had to be left to next day to set before you could cut it up cleanly. We used to get about ten bob for pig killing, but later on it went up to about a pound.

'Every year, a few days before Christmas, when there was a Lord Bagot at Blithfield Hall, we were asked to slaughter two beasts and cut them up for his lordship to give away to his tenants and staff. I think this finished in about 1936 or 1937.'*

As in so many villages, there used to be many more shops in Abbots Bromley. There were many more pubs, too – at least twelve in the nineteenth century. However, the number of pubs has at least remained constant throughout Victor's lifetime, there still being five. But he will not admit to having a favourite hostelry. Cannily, he comments: 'Don't forget they're all customers!'

When World War II started Victor continued to work with his father. At first there

---

*The Bagot family lived at Abbots Bromley for 400 years before building their hall at nearby Blithfield in the fifteenth century.

was little change, but 1940 proved to be a very difficult year, as Victor remembers:

'Rationing started when the big snow was on and there were drifts six feet deep. The council employed all these out-of-work men to dig people out. With the weather it was very difficult to get meat and sometimes we couldn't make deliveries. Another very cold year was 1947, but it wasn't so bad then for delivering as there were many more snow ploughs about. But they don't starve in the country – people could always get a boiling fowl from next door. Farmers always used to help each other out. Mind you, getting money from them is more difficult. They've always had three months credit. Dad did it, so I carried on – but I always knew they'd pay up; it was just that they had to wait till they sold something or the milk cheque came in.

'With the rationing, people had to register with you for a year and prices were set by the Ministry of Food, who sent through lists of price changes. Sausages, liver and hearts were not rationed but their prices were fixed. Rabbits became very popular and you could charge what you liked for those. We also used to sell rabbit skins to a gypsy couple who came out from Uttoxeter selling salt blocks and pegs. During rationing we didn't do any slaughtering and all animals were supposed to be sent to auction.'

From June 1942 to May 1946 Victor was in the RAF as an MT driver. This took him all over the UK, to Africa, Italy, Greece and the Far East. Fortunately he was never injured, but he had one near miss when an ammunition ship blew up in Italy: 'My lorry was full of holes. I put five or six of the injured in my vehicle and took them to hospital, and they were just the ones near me.'

Between 1948 and 1953 part of the nearby valley was flooded to create Blithfield Reservoir, and the large number of immigrant Irish workers who came into the area increased the Wilsons' business considerably. The workers lived on site in ex-army huts. Among the buildings flooded was the thatched lodge of Victor's grandmother. Victor remembers how, during the great drought of 1976, the old mill and some tree stumps which had been submerged came back eerily into view again.

In 1955, two years after his father died, Victor married the girl he had met in 1948. Mavis was from the Wirral, in Cheshire, and came to Abbots Bromley to teach at the village school. At first she thought Abbots Bromley was 'awful', but she soon settled down, to the extent that she has been a parish councillor for over ten years.

Today, Victor and Mavis find that the community spirit in Abbots Bromley – founded by the abbots of Burton – is almost as good as they ever knew it. 'It is a very friendly village where people still say good morning. It's not one of those places full of second homes, though there might be the odd one, and some people commute a long way to work in Birmingham or the brewery at Burton. Of course, there *have* been a lot of changes. You have a much better class of people livin' in Abbots Bromley now: it's all executive homes, and it's many years since I saw chickens and sheep in a house. Nobody comes in the shop any more and asks: "What can I have for a shilling?" Kids always used to walk everywhere, but now they always come by car and are well dressed.

'Apart from the fact that I've always lived here, I like Abbots Bromley because you can get out easily to many places. But it's a shame a lot of the shops and tradesmen have gone, including wheelwrights, builders and plasterers. Now you've got to go to Rugeley just for a tin of paint – in the old days any one of a number of fellers would have given

A village butcher's shop at the turn of the century. There would always be a wide range of products on sale – and almost as many people to serve the customers!

you half a pint. You can't even buy milk straight from the farm now.

'We used to have two bobbies, and the sergeant's front room was the police station. But you still had some crime. One day I'd gone early to the doctor's so my sister locked up and went home. Unfortunately, between us we forgot to take the till, as we usually did, and it was stolen in the night, though we didn't lose a lot. The funny thing was that we had a dog loose in the yard and it went for the police when they came to investigate, first thing in the morning, but it didn't go for the robbers. Perhaps it knew the thieves.'

Victor continued to slaughter animals until the late 1980s, although it wasn't something which he encouraged because it was often inconvenient and more trouble than it was worth. But it wasn't easy to disappoint old customers, so after he was married he would often 'get round' pig killing by pretending that new regulations had been introduced, preventing him from going out any more. Furthermore, slaughtering continued to be a heavy and often awkward task, even with the introduction of more humane methods. On one occasion Victor accidentally shot himself in the leg with a 'captive bolt' when a pig suddenly moved its head. Fortunately it missed the bone, and the wound itself was 'not too bad', but nevertheless it 'went wrong' and led to cellulitis, from which recovery was painfully slow.

Among the last few people for whom Victor slaughtered animals was local broadcaster/naturalist Phil Drabble, 'who used to bring in his free-range pigs for us to kill. Also, I used to go out to cull his goats in Bagot Woods.'

Victor retired at the age of sixty-seven and one of his four children, Simon, took over the business. He no longer lives 'above the shop', but on a small, modern estate up a nearby lane. Now he has more time for fishing and walking – but it is hard to break the habits of a lifetime, and for some time he continued to get up at five or six in the morning and help Simon with serving in the shop and delivering.

Wilson's is still very much a family business, with the emphasis on first-class service. Customer loyalty has been great, so it was not too surprising when, in 1995, a local farmer told Victor that he had not eaten anyone else's meat since about 1939! And a good reputation has always been very important in a close-knit community, especially with so many wagging tongues about. Mavis recalls: 'Men were always worse than the women, especially the farmers coming back from Uttoxeter market on a Wednesday.'

Although the population of Abbots Bromley has grown considerably during Victor's lifetime, to about 2,000, the number of businesses has declined sharply; yet the need to maintain standards remains strong. The village butcher must now compete with 'bargain' prices offered by distant supermarkets and larger meat retailers made easily accessible by modern transport. But cheapness is not everything: customers want consistency, quality, and sound advice too, and this is where the Wilsons really score. 'It's not just that much of the flavour's gone with the fat, but nowadays it's mostly boneless cuts sold, and that doesn't help the taste, either. Also, the meat's not matured enough now. Beef cattle must have a good age on the fields. Personally I can eat anything, but I don't have much lamb early in the year because the animals are too young and the old ones are well past it. You need to get through to Whitsun for English lamb, and then it's bootiful right through to summer.'

Perhaps the most unusual thing that Victor has supplied for the local community has been a pig's bladder for the jester's balloon in the annual medieval-dress horn dance. This takes place every September 'on the Monday after the first Sunday after the fourth, which means between the sixth and the twelfth'. A painting in The Crown Inn depicts the ancient festivity, in which dancers and musicians in Tudor dress commemorate the granting of hunting rights to villagers in Needwood Forest. In the dance, six men balance reindeer antlers on their shoulders, a seventh rides a hobby horse, and a 'fool' capers in multi-coloured motley; and they are accompanied by a boy with a bow and arrow, a girl, an accordionist and a triangle player. The antlers used (which hang in the church and never leave the parish) have been carbon-dated to about 1100, but the dance itself may be very much older. It could be that the horns have replaced other, earlier sets. But whatever the antiquity, the dance has never been more popular, the eager throng now being regularly swollen by parties of tourists. One year Victor had bladder balloons decorating his window and many of the visitors wanted them as souvenirs.

One evening, many years ago, an owl mysteriously appeared in Victor's shop, winking at him from a beam at the back. He admits that he had no idea where it came from and why it was there. In England, in recent centuries, it has been commonly believed that an owl entering a building foretells a death or very bad luck; but in Victor's case I like to think that, just as the horn dance has long brought prosperity to Abbots Bromley, so the owl signifies continuing success for the village's oldest butcher's. After all, many of the ancients, from the days when the horn dance started and long before, regarded the owl as the herald of good fortune.

A TRULY HELPING HAND

WILL JONES
Gardener of Shropshire and Lancashire

When young Billy Jones became garden boy on Shropshire's Pradoe estate his duties went way beyond digging and weeding. But then, in those days it was customary for almost everybody to 'put upon' the most junior of staff – the boy was even expected to empty his employer's lavatory, and this was no ordinary convenience, as Will recalls:

'The ol' man had his own personal privy in the garden, and as far as we knew he only ever went in it once a day, at 9am, when he walked round to see all the men. You'd only ever see him again at 2.30pm, but we don't think he ever visited the garden privy on his afternoon tour. Anyway, the back of this toilet was filled with sawdust, which the carpenter saved, and when the side handle was pulled the sawdust covered up "the business". Me and Sam Price the cowman had to empty it onto the farmyard manure about once a fortnight.'

Yet Will Jones never really minded even this unpleasant job because he was more than happy in his life and work. The estate where he was employed was very much at the heart of the local community; he was part of a village where 'everybody helped each other' and 'in any case, work was not work then'.

*The Pradoe estate in 1937. Note the kitchen garden (top right)
and the rose garden with its huge conservatory*

William Edwin Jones was born on 16 April 1908, at West Felton, in a lodge belonging to the Pradoe estate where his father worked as a farm labourer. He had three sisters, two brothers and 'plenty of good food, with home-grown potatoes, meat on Sundays, the odd hen, sometimes a roast rabbit – which I liked very much – a pig killed at Christmas, and two hams hung from the beams in the front room.' As well as raising six children, his mother worked in the estate laundry, attached to their cottage. According to Will, life was a lot better then:

'Everybody was happy, and there were no burglars about. Doors were never locked, and the coalman would let himself in. A few people had a free hundredweight of coal each year, and nobody ever knew where it came from; in fact we only found out when the vicar of West Felton died and it stopped. That wouldn't happen nowadays.

'People were always helping each other. They'd say: "If you're going into town, would you get me a bit of fish?", or whatever. And we'd all do the same. If a person had a horse and trap they'd think nothing of taking two or three dozen eggs into Oswestry market for you.

'Us schoolchildren always helped with the harvest; it was mostly smallholdings round here then, most with a cow, heifer and pig, and I'd rake the hay and cock it. But we were never given much pocket money for what we did because we were all neighbours and took turns to help each other. We had our treats, though. There was always a lovely

Sunday school summer tea party at Pradoe, when Mr Lloyd Kenyon, our landlord, would row us up the lake.

'If you were lucky you were given sixpence to deliver a telegram, and there were lots before telephones became common, especially with all the casualties during World War I. In the old days when a telegram came into the village post office the postmaster would find the nearest child to take it; but you'd have to wait to see if there was a message to bring back. That was the system everywhere in them days. Also during the first war there were no newspapers, so the post office put daily bulletins of war news in their window.

'Another thing we'd do was go tatta [potato] pickin' during the week's school holiday in October. And we'd pick blackberries all summer. Dealers used to come to certain places on certain days and give you a few coppers for what you had. A lot of the blackberries were used for dye, and so were damsons, but not so much.

'Sometimes we had to pick up the acorns at Pradoe to stop the cows – we had about thirty – eating too many. We sold some of them to Bradock's of Ruyton-Eleven-Towns; somebody said they were used to make gunpowder. But a lot of the acorns were taken by pigs – Hanley Hall had about sixteen porkers which were let loose when the acorns started, and they never went back till all the nuts were gone. They were always welcome on Pradoe's big lawn.

'Us lads could also earn a bit just after the first war, helping out with the shooting when it really got going again. Sometimes the gamekeeper would come up to the school and ask for six or seven beaters for a midweek shoot; the teacher didn't seem to mind, and we were pleased to get about half a crown each. Also, when we found a pheasant's nest we went to the gamekeepers. One would give us, say, a shilling, another 1s 6d. The keeper would take the eggs from all the nests reported and go round to the people on the estate to get about sixteen sitting hens to hatch them. He had all these different coloured rings to put on the hens' legs so that the broodies could all be identified and returned to their rightful owners when they were finished with. You'd often hear someone say: "Have you had your hen back, Mrs Roberts?" "Yes," she'd say, "and she's fat as mud." That always made me laugh.'

' The Foster Mother.'

But Will's childhood was not all fun and laughter. He remembers the discipline, too.

'I was one of about 140 kids of all ages at West Felton School, which now only takes juniors, and there was plenty of cane. Once I had four strokes. An old gent up the village had an orchard full of apples and he was fed up with them being taken, so he set a trap: he put tar on the back of the wall where we climbed over, and there was no water at school to wash it off; so when he came up the school in the afternoon we all had to show our hands, and five or six of us got caught out.

'Also, there were certain people who you had to salute, owners of small estates such as Mr Jacson of Tedsmore Hall; if we didn't salute him he'd tell your father or the schoolmaster, and then you'd be for it! If you met him at the end of the lane you'd have to salute, and even if you met him soon after at the other end, you'd have to salute him again. Sometimes you needed mechanical arms!'

On leaving school at the age of fourteen, Will went straight to Pradoe to work as gardener's boy for about 7s 6d a week plus meals. The estate also employed two full-time gardeners, a cowman, a bailiff, a gamekeeper, two estate men, and six maids, a butler and a cook in the house. The other gardeners had their own families and cottages, but young Will lived in at first, which meant he was conveniently on hand for many tasks.

The Kenyons were very charitable towards the staff and other local people. 'Sometimes Mrs Kenyon would come out with a tin of soup, and I'd have to take it up to anybody who was poorly in the village, even though this meant a walk of up to about a mile and a half. In winter Mrs Kenyon, Mrs Jacson and some other ladies used to come up to the school and make us kids a cup of cocoa, as there was no hot water there. But we had to pay a halfpenny for it.

'Every Christmas they used to kill a beast at Pradoe, and the bigger your family the bigger the piece of beef you were given. Also every year they'd kill five black pigs – never a white one, though I don't know why. Pradoe had its own slaughterhouse, but the local butcher came out to do the killing. Every house you went in in those days had the hams hanging up in muslin bags, and when you wanted some meat you just took the bag off and cut whatever you wanted. And when you cooked the bacon you had a pan full of fat, not all the water you get now.

'For curing the bacon we had big bars of salt, and it was always the kids' job to get the rolling pin and crush the salt fine before mixing it with saltpetre. You had to get it just right.

'When they killed a pig at Pradoe the postman would sometimes be given a lovely slice of pork pie. If not he'd always get a cup of tea and a slice of cake when he came at 9.30am and again in the afternoon.

'We grew a lot of gooseberries, and after we'd picked as many as were wanted in the big house, all the people on the estate were invited to come and pick the others off. And in about 1926, when there was no coal because of the General Strike, Mr Kenyon told everyone to go onto the lawn, which covered about a hundred acres including the lake, and gather up all the sticks for fuel. In those days the more people there were helping themselves to mushrooms or whatever, the happier the Kenyons were. Sometimes the lawn would be really busy on a Sunday evening, when people had a bit of time.

'The lake was well used, too. When us boys went out of school at twelve, for dinner, we'd go and jump in the water in the nude, and we'd do this all through the summer. The old man could see us through the window, but he'd never turn us off. It was all so different then.

'Sir Watkin Williams-Wynn's hounds used to meet at Pradoe, and the foxhunters used to come up to the front door for their drink. When they moved off, us workers were allowed to follow them as long as they were on Pradoe land, but as soon as they went onto the next estate we had to come back.

'Old Mr Kenyon was always good to me. One day, when I was about twenty, he said I ought to be confirmed – and I didn't mind because it meant I had two afternoons a week off to go to Ruyton-Eleven-Towns church for my instruction.'

Will's hours of work were 'about 8am to 5.30pm', and there was little chance of any staff being late as a maid at Pradoe was required to ring a bell 'at a quarter to eight for starting, at a quarter to one for lunch and half-past five for leaving off. In fact it was a very loud bell, and all the village people took their time off it.'

Gradually Will learnt the art and craft of gardening, how to supply Pradoe with flowers, fruit and vegetables in every season. He recalls that Mrs Kenyon was particularly fond of sweet peas in the house, and that within the kitchen garden they grew everything from peaches, pears and plums on the surrounding wall to strawberries, celery and asparagus in the beds. And of course, there was lots of lawn to mow. Will used a big machine pulled by a pony with leather shoes on to protect the turf, 'and you had to go straight as a die as old Mr Kenyon would soon tell you if you went off line.'

At the same time Will had to undertake innumerable other duties, both in the house and outdoors. Most were regular jobs, but others were one-offs:

'There were two pet swans, Nellie and Robert (named after Mr and Mrs Kenyon), which we had to get off the lake each winter and put in the shed so that the foxes couldn't get at them across the ice. But one morning Mr Kenyon missed the cock [cob] and the keeper and me were sent to look for him. We had to follow the brook all the way to Knockin, some three miles away, before we found him. Once we caught him we put him in a bag, with his head poking out through a slit we'd made. What a weight that was to carry all the way back! That's the sort of odd thing I was asked to do.

'First thing in the morning I has to take coal into the kitchen and empty it alongside the range, using a special little barrow. Then, if required, I had to take the trap to the station to fetch guests or things. We used to get tea in bulk, and a load of coal came by canal boat every month – though quite a lot was delivered. Harry Jones, the oilman, came every Friday and brought wooden barrels containing about fifty gallons of paraffin, as well as candles, matches and soap.

'The minute the Kenyons went on their summer holidays the main decorating and cleaning was done. All the lot of us had to drag out these heavy carpets onto the lawn, beat 'em out and drag 'em back in again. That was one of the worst jobs.

'At least I didn't have to cut the sticks for the bakehouse – that was the cowman's job. And sometimes he'd be there all day churning butter. But when the Kenyons held these big parties for local girls coming of age, such as the Sheas at The Grange, I was there for hours on end turning the handle to make ice-cream.

'Another regular job was getting logs for the house, though we did have a circular saw. Once we had an enormous lot to do when about a thousand trees were felled to pay off death duties. A lot of us used to burn wood shavings in our cottages: we used to go

The leaves had to be cleared from paths as well as lawns, a back-breaking and tedious task!

164

Horses used to work with the timber fellers in the forest, and it was often cruelly hard work for them, particularly when conditions were muddy and wet

down with a barrow and get the shavings from Deep Coppice, on Pradoe estate, where the clog makers worked for a long time. All the coalmen used to wear clogs.

'Also at Pradoe I had to see to the water, which came up to the house by means of a ram [hydraulic water-raising machine]; this would pump about twenty-four times a minute. Unfortunately I had to walk half a mile to switch it on, and half a mile back to switch it off; but it was lovely water.

'Another extra job we had to do was clear all the leaves off the gravel drive the week before Lenten service, which was midweek then. About four maids would go down to church, with Mr and Mrs Kenyon walking some way behind them. We always used to say that we had to clean the drive so that the maids could be heard walking with a boy, crunching on the gravel. It was very strict for the girls then.

'But I never used to mind what I did because I had a boss who was very kind to me. For a couple of years in the late 1920s I had to take Mr Kenyon out in a wheelchair each morning. But one day he said to me: "Willie, you're late!" I said: "Well sir, I haven't got a watch." And do you know, about a week later he got a lovely watch for me from Shrewsbury. And he'd always give me a ticket for Shrewsbury flower show and the police ball at Oswestry. He was good like that.'

Shropshire country life was very different in those days, with an agricultural system which was, in some ways, still fairly feudal. Will remembers it well:

'Rent day was twice a year, on 25 March and 29 September, when all the tenant farmers traipsed up to the big house with their money. Every manor was virtually self-sufficient and had its own blacksmith and joiner. We had three horses and a pony, and every month they would be shod, the smith doing a "remove" if the shoes were still good enough – that is, he took the shoes off, pared back the hooves, then nailed the same shoes back on again, each one onto the hoof it was on before. Everything possible would be done to save money.

'There was a local market every Saturday, but livestock were sold on Wednesday. Cattle and sheep were taken in from all over the place by drovers. Billy Hump was a good man and never lost an animal, but I don't know how he got his name.

'It was very hard work on the old farms. Someone would spend all afternoon just cleaning the soil off the mangolds and cutting them up in a machine for cattle feed. The thresher had five "mourners" who had no 'omes and followed the machine from place to place. They generally started at the end of October and just slept in the outbuildings, though each farmer had to feed them.

'At harvest we used to run the rabbits, knocking them on the head with sticks. But some of the farmers were very mean and I've been at a place where eighty were killed and we were never given one. So sometimes we used to hide one under a shock of corn and lay another on top. Then we'd know where it was and soon came back for it when the coast was clear. But at least when you worked for a farmer planting potatoes he would generally allow you to plant a row for yourself.

'We also used to longnet rabbits on a windy night, always working against the wind so that the rabbits couldn't hear you. I could always get a net out well. You almost had to run with the net-support sticks, to get the job done before any rabbits became suspicious and moved off. On a good night we'd run dozens into the net.

166

'There used to be a lot of cider apples and a cider mill in this parish. The cider was sold for about 2s a gallon, and at harvest the cider barrel would always be on the back of the wagon. A lot of people used to booze for days on end, and two of the worst were farmer Harry Jones and Dick Lewis the hedgelayer. Once they bored two holes in a haystack by the chapel and slept in these for over a week while they were on the beer, even though Harry's house was less than two miles away. No wonder his farm went to rack and ruin.

'A lot of the tenant farmers used to brew their own beer, taking it in turn, and passing the barm [fermenting froth] round to each other to save buying the yeast. This was fine as long as the barm was fresh.

'All my life we've had just the two pubs – The Fox and Hounds and The Punchbowl – in West Felton. I can remember when mild beer was only 5d a pint and bitter 6d. When there was a pheasant shoot at Pradoe the blacksmith used to see to the beer, going down to The Fox and Hounds for a small barrel. But when there was a partridge shoot I'd go down with the pony and trap to get a couple of dozen bottles of Worthington. They'd always serve us at The Fox and Hounds, even if they were officially closed.'

Despite all the beer drinking, Maddocks the village policeman appears to have had a quiet time in old West Felton. There was only one serious incident that Will can recall:

'John Dovaston owned a lot of land round here, and us kids were all scared of him. He wore a black cloak and we had to get off the path quick, out of his way, if we saw him coming. Then one day he shot a fellow in the leg just because his cattle got out and went into his crops. But somehow he got away with it.'

Will, too, occasionally resorted to the gun to resolve a problem, sometimes quite dramatically. Once he used his 20-bore hammer shotgun to shoot a rat in the scullery at Pradoe! On another occasion he used the same gun to 'shoot out a hornets' nest, a big ball under the eaves of the garden wall.' Unfortunately he was too close, and got stung on the head! In those days the cartridges were sent out with a bill from Ellis's of Oswestry.

'There were other pests to deal with, too', says Will. 'I had a lot of lovely cucumbers and one night they were all bit off. Rats turned out to be the culprits. There were rats and mice everywhere in the old days. Once

167

when I was in The Fox and Hounds talking to the gamekeeper I saw two mice come out of his feed bag, which he took everywhere.

'Another time I had a row of lovely peas and one morning about two yards had been eaten. I told the keeper and he put up a rabbit net, but what d'you think it was? Turned out to be a hedgehog, and what a job it was to get him out the net.

'There weren't the moles about then, but we caught a few. When we put their skins on boards to dry we used only little nails, so the holes weren't too big. When the oilman came on Friday he'd give us 6d or 9d for each skin.

'Another pest was jackdaws – they used to block up the chimneys at Pradoe with their nests. We used to call in Rogers, the sweep from Oswestry, twice a year: he came about five in the morning and it took him about half a day just to clean out the kitchen range.

'Foxes were a problem with the shoot, but Jones the keeper had a very effective alarm gun joined to a tape around the hens. I never knew what happened to that. We also had problems with poachers, and when we had a lot of partridges we put sticks out in the fields to stop the birds being netted.

'We didn't seem to get any trouble from gypsies, and only saw a few selling cottons and things. There were even fewer tramps as there were no workhouses (where the poor were given shelter and work) nearby. In some areas it was said they left marks for each other on roadside stones outside certain houses, with secret signs meaning such things as "You'll get nothing here", or "Beware of the dog".'

It was not surprising that some racial antagonism remained in this border country, even for an Englishman called Jones with a fair bit of 'Welshy' in his accent. For centuries Oswestry had been the centre of warfare between the English and Welsh. It was largely rebuilt in the nineteenth century, but old prejudices continued to be handed down from generation to generation, and these have been slow to disappear. As Will recalls, 'If you went to Oswestry in the old days and there were Welsh people standing in the street, you'd have to go round them. And once I went with the sheep drover back to his home, but his family ignored me and only spoke in Welsh; so I never went there again.'

In the 1930s Will became head gardener; he had also become engaged to Olive, the Kenyons' nanny – but all was not well at Pradoe. Will's original boss had died, and the 1,000-acre estate was now run by a new, very different generation of Kenyons. Once one of the maids was told off for being only two minutes late in after 10pm; and while the new boss was pleasant enough, he did not seem too concerned about the future. For

In Victorian times the head gardener was often responsible for overseeing the hot house as well as the outside work

example, Will recalls that 'the cellars had been absolutely full of wine bottles covered with cobwebs, but Mr Kenyon drank the lot and never replaced a bottle.'

Will and Olive left Pradoe in 1938 and went to live at Rochdale, where they married in 1939. Will was exempt from war service through having phlebitis, so he took a job as a chauffeur/handyman and was very happy in that position until he retired aged sixty-five. Then he played a lot of bowls and snooker and eventually found a part-time job as a chauffeur. However, over the forty-two years the Jones were there, Rochdale had become 'a horrible place', so in 1980 the couple were delighted to be given the opportunity to return to a rented cottage at Pradoe. Colonel John Kenyon had taken over from his father and was doing his best to inject new life into the estate, not least by starting to replenish the wine cellar!

Will with his wife, Jean

In 1988 ill health forced Will and Olive to give up their house at Pradoe, and they moved into a West Felton bungalow owned by Oswestry District Council. Colonel Kenyon remained a very good friend to them: 'He comes to see us nearly every Sunday and even sometimes struggles up here with a sack of potatoes for us!' Together they spent many hours mulling over how very different life used to be at West Felton.

On their return to the village after so many years, the Jones found many changes. Will describes the most obvious:

'Now there's only one shop instead of two, the fields have all gone to so many new houses, and the population has rocketed. There always used to be something going on, from whist drives to outings: I was on the committee of West Felton public hall from when it was built in 1923 till when I went to Rochdale. I acted as MC for all the dances, and I organised lots of sport. Now there's hardly any activity. Christmas isn't the same, either; before the war there wasn't a year when the handbells weren't played at Pradoe's door.

'At least Pradoe church is still going. It has the smallest parish in the country. Even Felton people, with their own church right by, still go to it. But Sunday doesn't seem to mean much to most people now. In the old days there was never any work on Sunday – you weren't even allowed to sew a button on, and you had to gather the sticks on Saturday for Sunday's fire.

'This is still a good village and we have good neighbours, but not so many people help each other now because they're not brought up to it. But at least we still have a few friends from our childhood nearby, to remind us of how good things used to be.'

Very sadly, Will Jones died on 4 December 1995, just a few weeks after I interviewed him. When he told me about the old days there was great enthusiasm in his voice and a wonderful sparkle in his eyes. I wish I had known him longer.

MASTER OF HIS OWN MUCK HEAP

PETER PEARL

Farmer and Policeman of Hampshire and Essex

Fourteen-year-old Peter Pearl was sometimes reduced to tears by his first job, but perhaps it helped to shape his character for the much more rewarding work which would dominate his life.

'I'd only ever thought about being a farmer. To me that was everything. But when I left school at Christmas in 1945 to work for Father I found myself all alone out in the middle of a twenty-acre field picking stones which could damage machinery. There were thousands of them, and you only needed two big ones to fill a bucket, so I sometimes sat down and cried at the hopelessness of it all. Then Mother gave me a little clock and I used to look at it and wish the time would go quicker when I sat down under the hedge to eat my bread and cheese. You couldn't have had a more soul-destroying job. But it did stand me in good stead for working alone as a country policeman, when I truly was master of my own muck heap.'

Peter's grandfather was a remarkable man, starting out as a humble road-sweeper for

West Suffolk County Council and ending up running a large Hampshire farm. Along the way he found time to father thirteen children, including Peter's father, whom he employed first as a haulage contractor carrying stone, later as a farm worker.

An only child, Peter Raymond Charles Pearl was born on 26 October 1931 at Over Wallop, near Andover in Hampshire. In December 1939 Peter's grandfather took a thousand acres of the Marquis of Winchester's estate at Monxton, near Andover; the family moved there because Peter's father was employed as a farm worker by his grandfather. Overall, Peter enjoyed a happy childhood in the Hampshire countryside, despite some vivid wartime memories:

'Most of all I remember what I looked forward to, especially my *Rainbow* comic and my Friday treat – a free funnel of sweets delivered with the basket of groceries to Nether Wallop by Mr Hawksworth.

'I was always helping Dad with his work, walking the horses round the well to draw water, putting corn into the troughs for cattle feed, cutting corn with the binder, making corn ricks, drawing the straw into yelms, (bundles laid straight) for thatching, and so on. During just one summer in the war Father thatched fifty-three ricks on Grandad's 1,000-acre farm.

'We never had a car then as we didn't go anywhere, but once in a while we did go on outings. The first time I saw the sea was in 1937 when I was six and we had a day trip to Bournemouth, where we took a steamer to Swanage. I didn't see the sea again for ten years, when I went to Mudeford. I was in a CC41 "utility" suit (with the official mark) and when I saw all these people in bathing suits I knew just how backward I was!

'I went to the village school at Wallop, then Highclere, then back to Wallop. But in 1940 Wallop school had to be evacuated because it backed onto the airfield, so some of us were sent to Abbotts Ann school while others went to Broughton. At Abbotts Ann

school we had two air-raid shelters, and when we were in them during raids we bagged up nettles for the war effort; I think they may have been wanted for their sugar content. While we did that we sang songs such as "My bonny lies over the ocean" and "Knees up Mother Brown".

'When I was eleven I went to Andover secondary modern boys' school, daily on a double-decker bus from Wallop. It was a long journey altogether because I also had to walk two miles across the fields from the house to the bus stop. Sometimes I helped Mum walk back with her shopping.

'One day on the school bus we

Posing proudly with their first car: Peter with his father and grandfather

had to stop and take shelter during a raid. Afterwards I saw the RAF men with hessian sacks shovelling up the remains of a German bomber crew in the road ahead. We also used to count the Spitfire squadrons in and out. "Only nine back today," we'd say.

'As well as the twelve full-time staff on his farm, Grandad had fourteen prisoners of war supplied by the Hampshire War Agricultural Committee. A couple of soldiers remained with their lorry all day, but usually they were well trusted and even drove tractors. The Italians were generally lazy but most of the Germans and Austrians worked like Trojans. When Grandad got this canvas-topped Austin 12-4 he loaded it up with lemonade and cigarettes for the POWS. They had a razor blade and used to cut each cigarette into three to make it last longer. The POWs couldn't believe how well they were treated and some became good friends. If anything broke down they were the first to help – one even fixed mother's clock.

'We ate quite well on the farm, as Dad was always going out bagging rabbits, pheasants and partridges. Rabbit pie was a great favourite.

'Grandad was a lay preacher and Dad was Church of England. Mother was in the choir at St Andrew's Church, Nether Wallop; and so was Bill Purdue, who smoked Churchman's cigarettes and gave me all the cards from the packets – one set was called "In Town Tonight" and had pictures of the stars of the day. During the services I used to sit down on the hassocks and look with wonder at these cards; I've collected them ever since.

'In those days postman Calloway at Wallop had a blue uniform with red piping; I remember how the top of his flat hat used to be soaked with sweat as it was such hard work delivering all those parcels on a bike. At Monxton the postie had to cycle three

miles out to our farm.'

In 1947 the Pearls suddenly decided on a change of direction. 'One day Father told me: "You're not going to work as I did for Grandad: we're going to have a farm of our own." Then Grandad got to hear of this and sold Dad 120 acres of arable at Middle Wallop. Father had no money to spare for the £500 purchase so he borrowed it from the bank, who then provided a further £1,500 for development, with the farm itself as collateral. He repaid the lot in two years! Using secondhand materials, my uncle built Dad a bungalow on the "new" farm, and later on my wife and I moved into it. Meanwhile Dad had built another bungalow nearby.'

As well as helping his father with their chickens and herd of dry (beef) cattle, Peter did a lot of ploughing for cereal production. As a result, he became very proficient with his Fordson Major and in 1951, at the age of seventeen, won first prize with his trailer plough in the Wallop Growmore Club competition. He was also a member of the Wallop Growmore quiz team and remembers what an adventure it was when they went 'all the way to Binstead, near Alton, in the dark!' The only other regular excursion was the Tuesday run to Salisbury market, where he enjoyed the company of other young farmers; but he did not usually drink there, 'as Grandad didn't approve'.

Peter's first recollection of a village policeman is of one coming out to the family farm to sign the cattle register. The local bobby was required by law to check records of all cattle movements, as part of his work in preventing and containing livestock disease. Through such contact

1950 Fordson Major tractor advert

The Pearls cutting the winter oats in 1950

Peter came to admire the Wallop policeman, whom he regarded as 'very upright, efficient and hardworking, someone who commanded respect'. Sometimes he went to visit him at home, and one day he said to Peter: 'Why don't you join up?' But Peter said: 'No, I don't want to leave Dad.'

However, after Peter married Margaret in 1955, he was persuaded to join the Hampshire and Isle of Wight Special Constabulary at Andover. He still lived at Monxton and worked on the farm, as specials were not paid; he was attached to the Wallop policeman whom he had admired so much. However, Peter describes what happened next, a tragedy which changed his life completely:

'For a couple of years I used to float around and fly the flag when it was officer Jim Dolan's rest day. We had what were called "duty scales", where we'd register a route with the station so that they knew which telephone box to ring when they wanted you. However, expected arrival times were not too reliable when you were out on your bike wearing the cape in a headwind, with punctures to contend with. But generally you managed to make your patrol points, noting anything suspicious along the way. Sometimes I did odd things such as attend the local flower show. Once I even went to a house to help with a big two-day furniture sale. I also did a bit of traffic control, for which you needed eyes in the back of your head.

'Suddenly Jim Dolan was posted to Weyhill, near Andover, and I thought: "Oh my God, my friend's gone". Then one night Jim was called out to check vehicles for a stolen car. Unfortunately, as he stood in a main road in his dark uniform he was hit in the back by a car whose driver hadn't seen him, and was thrown into the path of the vehicle he was attempting to stop. Even more sadly, he was killed by a person he knew.

'In some strange way this spurred me on to join the police full-time. At the time we had our first child and I was only on poor wages. Farming had been good during the war with home production at a premium, but with the decline that followed the only alternative to expansion was going under. So one day I went over to Andover police station and asked to join. When I did so the sergeant nearly fell out of his seat, because only rarely did people who had been specials want to be regulars.

'However, after I had taken the exam I was turned down on account of my height, being only 5ft 9in when Hampshire then wanted men of 5ft 10in. So I tried Dad's old county, West Suffolk, where they usually took men as short as 5ft 8in – but then it is flat country! To my surprise, I had a letter back saying they'd already accepted too many at my height and had temporarily pushed the height up to 5ft 9½in. So I was bitterly disappointed again.

'But I was determined to get in, so I went to Andover to see the local inspector whom I knew quite well, as I had supplied manure for his garden. He suggested that I tried Essex police as he knew the force there and they only wanted 5ft 8in. So after passing a written examination, I went off to Chelmsford for interview with Captain Peel, who had been chief constable since 1933; he was a direct descendant of Sir Robert Peel, who reorganised the London police force and gave rise to the terms "bobby" and "peeler" for a policeman. When Captain Peel found out I was from Wallop he was most impressed, and when I told the panel I delivered manure to the inspector they laughed their heads off. That afternoon I passed the medical, and I was officially accepted the very next day.

'I trained at Eynsham Hall, Oxfordshire, then the centre for several police forces. But whereas marching to music was easily managed by most of the other recruits because they'd been in the forces, it was very strange for me. The training sergeant used to say to me: "Come on Pearl, you haven't got a pitchfork in your hand now." Altogether I found the thirteen weeks training very hard going as I'd had a very sheltered existence back on the farm.

'My first posting was to South Ockendon, near Grays, which was a village with industry and a London-overspill area, but a good place to start a career as I was thrown in at the deep end and given bags of experience. However, I still stood out like a sore thumb with my broad Hampshire accent.'

One major change for Peter was a considerable rise in income. Back on the farm he had only been getting about £5 a week, and as a volunteer special all he received was a boot allowance. But as a full-time, fully trained policeman he earned a weekly wage of £13 8s 4d gross, £9 13s 5d nett, and he still has that first payslip – for 31 May 1958 – to prove it. After two postings, Peter had two ambitions: to be a village policeman and to earn the long-service and good conduct medal. At twenty-nine he was very young to take on a village alone, yet he was posted to Kelvedon Hatch, near Brentwood. There he spent the two hardest years of his life, but it was also an interesting and rewarding time.

'I was based in the first countryside you get to on the way out of London so I had no end of work with poachers, and the duty periods were very tiring, especially the one from 5am to 8am. One morning I saw a dairy-man walking to work along a country lane, and that evening the chief superintendent paid me a surprise visit and asked me what I'd seen that day. I said "Only a dairyman on his way to work, sir." But he said: "Ah, that's good: he'll go into the pub tonight and tell people he saw the policeman. There's nothing like showing the flag." And I must agree.

'One morning in early 1963 a farmer said he had poachers and picked me up in his Land Rover. When we got to his farm we saw three figures in the distance, sunlight glinting on gun barrels, and a black dog. "There they are," the farmer said, "and they've no right to be there." So he dropped me off to apprehend them while he went for further assistance. As I walked up this lane I heard voices and looked up to see them coming through the spring wheat, about 200 yards away. Nearby was a motor car. I noted its detail and also a cartridge belt in the back window. These chaps were well dressed in brogues and suits, and said they had permission

PC Pearl in Kelvedon in 1963

from the farm nearby, but they were not aware of the boundaries. So I took their guns and bandoliers and reported them for poaching offences.

'The men were duly convicted of poaching, but as they did not have game in their possession they got their guns back. Little did I realise that two of them were to become household names in connection with the Great Train Robbery that August; their conviction for poaching was their last before the famous event took place. As a result I helped the detectives on the big case and we revisited the scene of the poaching, though nothing was found. It seemed that the men *had* simply been poaching when I accosted them, and quite honestly, I couldn't see what harm they'd done that day. They were most impressed when they got their guns back in good condition as they obviously valued them quite highly.

'We also used to get a great many horse-drawn gypsy caravans in the area, and were inundated with complaints from the parish council. One day when I went to their camp there was this lady with a string of washing out and making artificial flowers. When I confronted her she said: "We don't need permission to camp here, we're gypsies." And she added: "I can't go, sir, as I've a child in hospital," which was always a favourite excuse. But Britannia Smith was clearly in the wrong, and was taken to court for parking along the highway.

'Another time a local landowner complained that the gypsies had been stoning his cows, so I went and seized these two boys' catapults. Their father was another one who pleaded: "We can't go, sir, as we've a child in hospital."

'A while later I was at the landowner's house and there was a relative of his there, a well-known politician, who said: "You British policemen do an exceptionally fine job; I'm going to bring this up in the house." He'd obviously been told that we managed to move the gypsies on again – but what he didn't know was how we did it. My sergeant had shown them a piece of blue paper which they took to be a form for their arrest as they couldn't read. But we said: "If you go within the hour we haven't seen you." You haven't seen anybody move so fast in your life, and as they went one of them – Leafy Low – said: "You're gentlemen policemens, sir, you really are."

'Generally I always had a good relationship with the the gypsies; they always treated me with respect and called me sir or constable, and I was always happy to sit round their fire drinking a mug of cocoa – yet next day, by way of total contrast I'd be talking to some gentleman by the fireside in some great house. The only really serious incident I remember involving gypsies was when I had to help out at Ongar show and a lot of them were drinking there. In the evening some of them were driving like mad around the pub car park back in my village and I had to jump on the running board and pull the keys out of the ignition to make them stop. Then half a dozen of them set on my special and me. And later on a man from one gypsy faction nearly severed the arm of a rival when he pushed it through a car window. They came to the house and Margaret had to rip up a sheet to make a tourniquet.'

At Kelvedon Hatch, Peter had a list of livestock owners and he was required to sign their registers every three months, to make sure that all animal movements had been recorded. It was also a good way for him to get to know people, though not everybody kept to the letter of the law. Peter recalls one man in particular:

'I went to see a livestock keeper of Church Lane, but was very surprised by what I found. There was this small, dirty bungalow surrounded by high nettles, and nearby a little galvanised building with a wooden cross, all badly needing repair. When I knocked on the door it was answered by a lady in her nineties, wearing a black hat with a big pin through. I said: "I'm the new policeman." "Oh", she said, "have we done anything wrong? I'll get my son." Then out came this man wearing a green pork-pie trilby hat, a jumper with a hole where the belt had frayed through, and an old grey jacket. He was just like a character from Dickens.

'This gentleman said to me: "I knew your predecessor. He was a very good man and gave me a lift when I wanted it." "What, in his car?" I asked. "No," he said, "with a coffin. Would you be able to help me if I need it? Also, I wonder if you would recommend me to people who need my services."

'Then I asked him to get his cattle register, and it was in a terrible mess, not having been completed for two years. After that I asked if he had a chapel of rest for his undertaking business. "Yes," he said, pointing to the dilapidated corrugated iron building engulfed by undergrowth. "Could I have a look?" I said, "I've never been in a chapel of rest before." "I'm afraid it's inconvenient," he replied, "as I'm rearing some turkeys in it for Christmas"!

'So I told him to get his register made up and then I left; and my wife went to Brentford and bought the official movement book, which I gave him. It turned out that he was a single man who lived there with his mother and sister. At a later date I saw him "in action", when he wore a black frock coat which appeared green with age. But he was a most agreeable, sincere man and I had a lot of time for him.

'When I went to my first sudden death on that beat he was the only undertaker I knew, so I recommended him to the relatives. But he rolled up in a pale-blue, ex-Frigidaire Dormobile to collect the body and I had to help him get it on board! Then he said: "Put your bike in with the coffin and I'll give you a lift!" But I really couldn't do that, as the relatives were looking out of the window. "OK," he said, "You follow me round the corner and load up when we're out of sight," which we did.

'On another occasion I cut my finger badly when carving the Sunday joint, but Margaret couldn't take me to the local doctor to have it stitched up because she didn't drive at that time. The only person we knew who could get me there was the undertaker, so we phoned him and he took me over in his blue undertaker's van! When the doctor asked how I had got to him, I had to reply: "The undertaker brought me."'

One day the rector of Kelvedon Hatch asked Peter to serve on the parochial church council. Peter readily agreed, but he had to be confirmed first. Peter particularly remembers one Christmas Eve when he was on point outside the church:

'It was snowing like hell and this car drew up. Out came my inspector, Payne from Chipping Ongar, and he said, "I've just come out to wish you a happy Christmas and sign

your pocket book." Then he asked: "What's going on over there?" and I replied "Midnight service, sir." Then he said: "Well, let's go over and join them," so we did. That was a time I will never forget. So was my last day in Essex, when chief constable John Nightingale bothered to pay me a surprise visit in the village, to say goodbye. He wished me well, and told me always to remember that Essex had trained me.'

In 1963 Peter was accepted for transfer to his native Hampshire. After two years at Romsey, Peter was posted some ten miles away, to the village of Broughton, where he would remain for twenty-two years and become the longest-serving rural beat officer in the Hampshire and Isle of Wight Constabulary. This was all the more remarkable because Peter's birth certificate was registered at Broughton, and it was unusual for someone to be posted near to his birthplace.

Immediately Peter noticed how very different the villagers were from people in the areas where he had been working; he found them a very introverted community, and began to realise how much *he* had changed. The Pearls also found that the 1931 house – one of the three oldest police houses in Hampshire – was small compared to the one they had left behind in Romsey. Furthermore, because there was no proper office, the children had to leave the sitting room whenever there was a knock at the door and Peter needed to take a statement, or help a road accident victim with cuts and bruises, or issue a pig licence to a farmer in muddy boots, and so on. And if Peter was out on duty his superiors knew they could always get hold of Margaret to initiate things, unlike today when many of the police officers' wives are out at work. Yet Broughton was a place the Pearls soon came to love: the children went to the local school, and the whole family gradually became very involved in many village activities, not least the drama group.

During Peter's time there, Broughton had a very stable population of about a thousand, mainly farming folk; however, the number of shops fell from six to one. His beat also included the village of Houghton and the smaller parishes of Bossington and Buckholt. Unfortunately the area had two fast main roads through it, bringing many accidents, as Peter recalls:

'Two of the worst places were on the A30, at Leonard's Grave and Nine Mile Water, described by one local solicitor as "a crossroads for the quick or the dead". But at first I wasn't always that prompt to get on the scene because all I had was the pushbike, a Raleigh three-speed of my own but which I had an allowance for. Therefore I often had

Thatching a wheatrick:
one of the crafts to which Peter was accustomed before joining the police

181

to rush out, stop the first vehicle passing and ask the driver to take me to the scene. Fortunately I generally had good co-operation.

'From 1968 I could get to accidents much quicker because I was given a grey Velocette motorbike with a water-cooled engine. It was known as a "Noddy bike" and I had to share it with the Wallop policeman. Neither of us had driven motorbikes before and we were just told to get a provisional licence and to practise up and down the road outside the police house. I finished up with a Honda, which was much more powerful. Unfortunately, having a motorbike and radio meant that I was easily called upon by Winchester HQ and despatched to incidents over a much wider area.'

There were plenty of other sudden deaths to deal with too, through natural causes, accidents and suicides. Here Peter describes how he had to deal with this sort of thing:

'A retired gardener in the village, old Charlie, was missing from his wardened flat for over a week and I walked everywhere looking for him, even along the River Test. Then two lads offered to help look for him – and it wasn't long before one of them came running back with his face white as a sheet. He'd found Charlie in a 22,000-gallon water tank up on stanchions. It appeared that he'd climbed the ladder, kicked it away, climbed in, closed the lid with a wire and drowned himself. When I looked in the first thing I saw was his grey cap, which I knew well. He was floating but I just couldn't get him out so I went back home for my daughter's skipping rope, and this did the trick when the sergeant arrived and gave me a hand. Inside Charlie's jacket was a tin containing his pocket watch and it had stopped at two o'clock, just ten minutes after he had last been seen.

'One young man had taken his life with a shot in the stomach simply because he was worried about his car insurance following an accident.

'One of the saddest things I remember dealing with was when I had to tell a wife and mother I knew that her husband had passed away in hospital after a massive coronary. She asked me to say a prayer there and then, which I readily did, and that was the most poignant moment in my career: it was then I realised that you had to be deeply understanding to be a good policeman.'

Animals, too, sometimes needed Peter's assistance. In 1967 he rescued a dog which had fallen down a dry well at Dunbridge. To find out the depth, Peter dangled a rope down, pulled it up and measured it on the ground: it was over 30ft. The only way he could get down was to strap two ladders together, which he did, and the dog was returned safely to the surface. Later he was awarded the RSPCA's bronze medal 'for courage and humanity' – but he got into trouble with his boss for not calling out the fire brigade!

Every year, when Peter was on parade, Lord Louis Mountbatten asked him why he was wearing that RSPCA medal on the right and not the left. Each time Peter told him: 'Because it's a civilian award, my lord.' Nonetheless he had great respect for the Queen's uncle: 'He was a wonderful man. Sometimes I was one of the police officers who went to his Broadlands home when there was a security alert, and then he always made us feel at ease, often inviting us inside.'

Among the more unusual people Peter had to deal with was a man who did a lot of walking; he was always handing in pound notes he found along the way, for which Peter would give him receipts, and after a month or so the man would be given any unclaimed money.

Much more eccentric was a lady who imagined she had rats in the roof. 'She kept on asking me what I was going to do about it so I went round just to keep her happy. She'd put rat poison everywhere, even over the furniture. "Can you hear them?" she asked. "No," I replied, but I did say that I would ask the council to check. When I did so they said: "Oh, we know all about that lady."

'After a while she complained to my boss that I hadn't done anything about the rats, and eventually she came in with a letter from Harold Wilson at Number 10, demanding action. So I telephoned the environmental officer. When they heard that I'd called about this lady I was told that he was out; but when I said I had a letter from the prime minister he was suddenly in.

'As a result, a man was sent out with a bag of ordinary flour, a spoon and a stick to make her think something was being done. But then the woman accused the poor pest controller of trying to poison her, so he came scurrying back to my wife with the flour saying that he was going to keep it as evidence in his defence! She never stopped complaining about the rats until eventually she was moved to a flat.'

At Broughton, Peter only used his truncheon once, to break a window to get into a house whose elderly lady owner had not been seen for a while. But he did use his handcuffs a few times, once quite unnecessarily. He describes what happened:

'A local man had entered into an agreement with a family to buy a typewriter, and

An agricultural accident

they accused him of stealing it when he went away. So Strathclyde police arrested him and I was sent in plain clothes, on the plane, all the way up to Scotland to collect him. There was the most tremendous fuss. I even had to bring the typewriter back and accompany the man to the toilet on our journey. It was the only time I've ever been to Scotland and I was only there for half an hour – in the dark! Then, after all that trouble and expense, when the man appeared in court next day he was acquitted after the magistrate said he had a legal right to the typewriter. And we'd only bought a single air fare for him!'

Sometimes Peter had to deal with hardened criminals who showed no compunction in stealing from the church. He recalls two cases involving remarkable audacity:

'After a spate of thefts from country churches we were circulated with a description of a suspect and I took the details down to the rector at Broughton.

'A few months later the rector came to see me and said that he'd just passed a man walking along the road and he fitted the description. Also, the ladies cleaning the brass had recently reported a strange man in the church. So I rang Stockbridge station and asked for a car, and we got over to the remote church of Bossington as quickly as possible.

'We parked the car and crept out, and as we were walking down towards the church a rotund man with a rolling gait came along the path. "Good morning," we said, and he replied "Good morning officers: what a lovely morning." We asked him what he was up to, and he said that he'd wanted to visit the church but it was locked so he was going to get the key. He added that he was a Methodist minister from Farnham and was very interested in old churches; but we were suspicious, because the time of day he was there didn't tie up with the bus timetable. Then he asked if he could see the church, and we said he could. As we walked along we enquired about his rolling gait and he said he had been a padré in the first war. But that didn't seem right, either, because he was too young and we thought he was carrying some considerable weight.

'After that we said we were not satisfied with his explanations and told him that we were going to search him. "How dare you insult a minister of the cloth," he said. Then we undid his jacket, and under his jumper was a rope with the most amazing conglomeration of antique church keys all round it. "OK, the game's up," he said. Then we asked him what he had done that day, and he admitted that he had been to King's Somborne church and drunk the communion wine.

'Later we discovered that the man was actually wanted for stealing petrol; he was even drawing on someone else's pension book, and had a string of convictions going back to 1921. In short, it was a good "nick", and it showed excellent co-operation between the village bobby and the rector, as well as how crucial the alertness of the cleaning women had been.

'But sometimes people are too trusting. One day the vicar of Houghton found a man asleep in the church porch, felt sorry for him and let him in. After the morning service it was found that the offertory box attached to a pew had been rifled. The vicar called me out, and I discovered that at the service there'd been only three people, all of whom were known. I asked what was likely to have been in the box and the vicar said that one of the regular worshippers usually rolled up a ten-shilling note and put it in. So I rang

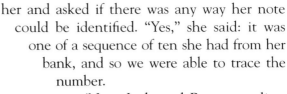

her and asked if there was any way her note could be identified. "Yes," she said: it was one of a sequence of ten she had from her bank, and so we were able to trace the number.

'Next I phoned Romsey police, gave them the vicar's description of the suspect, and said that the vagrant was probably walking along the road from Houghton to Mottisfont with the stolen money in his pocket. So off they dashed – and picked him up. He even had the ten-shilling note still rolled up in the fashion it was put in the box. Subsequently, not only was he charged with theft, but also sacrilege, breaking and entering a divine place of worship: he got three months.'

Other villagers had a surprisingly indifferent attitude to crime prevention, not least the late landlord of The Greyhound at Broughton. When Peter was carrying out a survey he asked the licensee what his security system was. He replied: 'Oh, I got a good one. I have a loaded shotgun and if I heard anyone I'd rush upstairs and I'd fire it out the window. The man from the garage would hear it and he would phone the police.' This was because the inn had no telephone.

When Peter first arrived in the village he went into the pub just after drinking-up time, at about 11.15pm, to encourage a little respect for the law, as 'last orders' were being called too late. Not surprisingly, for a time he was regarded as a 'hot copper'. Nevertheless, there were many occasions when Peter had a good laugh with the villagers, not least through his involvement with television. Here he explains how this came about:

'Southern Television filmed a large part of the *Wurzel Gummidge* series at Broughton, and I was required to be on hand to control the traffic and so on. I had permission to do this, the TV company paid for my services, and when I helped out my normal police work was covered by someone else. The local children were always allowed out of school to watch, and in the afternoon the TV crew would give them tea and buns.

'One day the crew adapted the local post office to their liking and I was standing there with my bike, cycle clips and helmet, talking to Wurzel who was played by actor Jon Pertwee. Suddenly, into the village came a van with "Bowyer's Wiltshire sausages" painted on the side, on its way to deliver to the village shop. I approached the driver and said: "Shhh, switch the engine off, please." At that, the driver said: "What the . . .'s going on?" Then over came Jon Pertwee and said: "It's all right matey, we's only doin' a bit of wangling" (angling). That was enough for the driver! "Bloody hell," he said: then reversed, and I didn't see him again that day. He must have thought we were a right lot, me with my bike and all, looking like a character from the set!'

There were even a few lighter moments resulting from road accidents, as Peter recalls:

'Once, when a car was travelling too fast and hit a tractor, one of my witnesses was the comedian Cyril Fletcher. In court the magistrate asked the tractor driver how long he'd been driving. "I've been drivin' tractors all my life, sir," he replied, and Cyril whispered to me: "That'll make a good line; I must remember that."

'Another time, after an accident on the A30 the people with injuries were taken off by ambulance. But when I was clearing up on the road I found a budgie in a cage, which one couple had been taking on holiday. So I put it between my knees on the motorbike and took it home. Later I phoned the people at Winchester hospital and told them I'd look after their bird till they were discharged. When they came to collect it they were really pleased, and even resumed their holiday.'

A poaching incident, too, seemed funny at first, but had a surprising link with a more serious crime. Peter describes what happened:

'One night when we were out after poachers at Horsebridge, near Houghton, I heard this "pad pad" of someone running along the road. When the figure approached I jumped out and shone my torch in the face of this gypsy. "And what are you up to?" I enquired. "I missed the bus, sir," he said. But when I challenged that he changed his mind and said he was "took short". So I searched him and found a catapult plus lovely round pebbles for ammunition. Unfortunately he wasn't carrying any game so nothing could be proved, but I took his catapult and pebbles and gave him a receipt.

'Nine months later Southampton police were investigating a burglary and found a jacket at the scene; inside it was my receipt for one catapult and six pebbles. They asked me if I could identify the person. "Yes," I said, and took them to the place where the man worked. As soon as he saw me he said "Hullo, Mr Pearl," and he was arrested on the strength of that little bit of paper which he'd kept all that time.'

Another of Peter's stories illustrates the importance of the village bobby's role as mediator when people become incensed by relatively trivial things:

'A man who lived near the goal at the local playing field kept getting the football in his garden, and would keep it. Despite pleas from the players, he would only ever return it to PC Pearl, so they were always having to stop the match and send for me. Eventually the man got really fed up with all this because he had a lovely garden and he didn't want it threatened by anybody or anything. So he put a garden prong through the ball, and I had no choice but to apply the full rigour of the law.

'Even after that it looked as if the antipathy would continue, so I suggested a meeting, as a result of which a high net was put up. Fortunately this solved the problem. Diplomacy, as in so many aspects of life, was the name of the game.'

There were quite a few retired service officers in and around Broughton, and some insisted on calling Peter by his surname. Such formality was by then unusual among the villagers, but it reflected much earlier times, when policemen generally were lower down the social scale. As an example of this: during the late nineteenth century a party was held by the staff at a large village house, to which the Broughton policeman was invited. But when the owner found out he took umbrage and complained to the chief constable; the bobby was fined about 15s, then a week's wages, and dismissed the service. Such a tough régime continued well into this century. Indeed, between the wars, when Broughton was part of the New Forest police division, the constable still had to cycle the twenty-three miles each way to collect his weekly pay!

During the great storm of October 1987 a tree fell on the Pearls' police house, just a couple of days before Peter was due to retire. Nobody was injured but the family certainly regarded it as an omen: it was the end of an era.

Not surprisingly, Peter was made a freeman of the village he had served so well. The man who had spent over two decades doing everything from seeing children safely through the streets on their way to harvest festival, to putting up cyclists with nowhere to stay, was retiring to nearby Romsey. He is justly proud of his record; as he stressed, 'In a village you're not just a man in uniform. The people see you in "civvies", too, and both you and your family always have to set an example.'

ACKNOWLEDGEMENTS

Most of all I wish to thank the wonderful people who are the subjects of my book, for allowing me to delve so deeply into their fascinating lives, for allowing me to reproduce their precious old photographs and documents, and for their kindness and hospitality. Also many thanks to all their spouses and relatives who have helped me in so many ways. A special thank-you to Reverend Fred Pennington for allowing me to use extracts from his fascinating book *From Ploughboy to Priest*, which is available from him at Sunset Cottage, West Street, Hartland, Devon, EX39 6BQ. In addition I wish to thank Mr B. Segrave-Daly and Steve Manning of Adnam's Brewery, Bass Taverns, Rene Bradshaw, Ken Beattie, Virginia Bunyan, Ann Fitzgerald of the Post Office, Denis Heard, Colonel John Kenyon, Maureen Lee, Tony Manley, Steve Metcalfe of Sussex Police, Don Phillips, Christopher Pope of Eldridge Pope, Robin Rolfe, Reverend Rod Sanders, Surrey Police, Hugh Sacker, John Sutton, Gillian Turner, Dr Waldron-Lynch, David Woodhouse and N. J. Sellick of Hall & Woodhouse (Brewers) Ltd and Peter Young of Hampshire Police. I am further indebted to the following publications: *Amateur Gardening*, *Church of Ireland Gazette*, *Country (CGA)*, *Country Quest*, *Country Living*, *Farmer's Weekly*, *The Grocer*, *Ireland's Own*, *Irish Medical Times*, *Irish Times*, *Scottish Farmer* and *Shooting Times & Country Magazine*. Finally, sincere thanks to my editor, Sue Hall of David & Charles, and to my wife Carol for her help in many ways.

INDEX

Page numbers in *italics* indicate illustrations

Abbots Bromley, Staffs, 150–8, *151*
Accidents, 8, 28, 35, 36, 46, 57–8, 70, 71, 76, 98, 128, 141, 142, 175–6, 180, 181–2, *183*, 186
Acorns, 161
Admaston, Staffs, 152
Aeroplanes, 57–8
Aga cookers, 75
Albion Hotel, Wimborne, 50–1, 56
Allotments, 25
Allowances, 43
Almshouses, 118
Anaesthetics, 78
Anderson, Miss May, 140
Animal cruelty, 46, 154
Animal cures, 128
Animal diseases, 41, 75
Avery, Dick and Lewis, 93
Ayrshire, 134–5

Babycham, 54
Bagot, Lord, 153, 154
Bakers, 18, 64, 65, 66, 71, 116, 126, 144, 152, 164
Balsdon, Harry, 97
Bar codes, 66
Battle, Sussex, 36, 40, 47
Beagles, North Bucks, 26
Beating the bounds, 146–7
Beckley, Sussex, 47
Bedford, 19
Beer, 48–60, 91, 94, 167
Beith, Ayrshire, 134

Bells, 20, 27, 113, 163, 170
Belper, Co Meath, 74–81
Betjeman, John, 30
Bexhill-on-Sea, 32, 33, 36, 46
Bicycles, 16, 21, 28, 32, 33, 34, 64, 75, 102, 115–16, 173–4, 177, 181–2
Bideford, Devon, 94
Birmingham, 116
Bishop, Emma and Bill, 51, 52, 53
Black Horse, The, Sturminster Marshall, 48–60, 52
Blacksmiths, *10–11*, 15, 26, 62, 112, 116, 166
Blandford, Dorset, 51
Blithfield, Staffs, 154
Borders, The, 134–45
Bores, 58–9
Bossington, Hants, 181, 184
Bournemouth, 54, 172
Brandy, 91
Bread, *see* Bakers
Brecon Beacons, 62
Breweries, 13
Bradford, Devon, 104
Breconshire, 61–71
British Legion, 30, *30*
Broughton, Hants, 180–7
Brownies, 132
Buckholt, Hants, 181
Buckinghamshire, 14–30
Buckland Monachorum, 126–33
Bucks Mills, Devon, 109
Bullock, Dr James, 144

Burials, *see also* Funerals, 102
Burleigh, Lord, 38
Burrow, Thomas Cory, 91
Buses, 46, 139, 140, 172
Butchers, 8, 62, 97, 112, 116, 144, 150–8, *153*, 156, 162
Butter, 65, 66, 70, 94, 164

Candles, 158, 164
Cann, Sam, 91
Carol singing, 20, *20*, 21, 99
Carpenter, 112, 116, 166
Carriages, 23
Cars, 16, 23, 34, 41, 45, 49, 54–6, 60, 67, 71, 75, *77*, 80, 106, 112, 122, 139, 172, *173*, *178*, 182
Carts, 18, 64, 75, 76, 152, *153*, 153, 160, 164, *191*
Catapults, 186–7
Cats, 63, 92
Catsfield, East Sussex, 31–47
Chapel, 65, 93–4, 112, 133, 173
Charity, 126, 162, 170
Charlbury, Oxon, 117
Chauffeurs, 22–3, 47, 51, 170
Cheese, 56–7, 66, 67
Chemists, 77
Chickens, 64, 94–5, 116, 127, 153, 154, 161, *161*
Children, 12, 20, 26, 32, 66, 87, 130, 160
Chimney sweeps, 168
Choirs, 19–20

Christmas, 20, 24, 26, 52, 54, 59, 65, 67, 92–3, 94, 95, 99, 104, 130, *139*, 140, 145, 153, 154, 160, 170, 180
Church, 8, 16, 18, 26, 27, 28–9, 30, *40*, 41, 45, 55, 64, 65, 74, 75, 79, 86–109, *93*, 112, 113–14, 115, 116, 117, 132, 133, 134, 136, 137, 138, 140, 145, 146, 148, 151, 160, 163, 165, 173, 180, 184–5
Churchwardens, *40*
Cider, 94, 97, *166*, 167
Cigarettes, 54, 60, 66, 173
Civil defence, 34
Class system, 118, 187
Cleaning ,14–30, 52, 164
Clergymen, *see* Church
Clogs, 165
Clothing, 19, 23, 25, 30, 32, 35, 43, 67, 143, 165, 176
Clovelly, Devon, 109
Coaches, 55–6
Coal, 64, 160, 162, 164, 165
Cobblers,19, 62
Cockfighting, 137
Cocktails, 54
Colchester Technical College, 95
Comics, 172
Commercial travellers, 67
Communications, 45
Community spirit, 7, 15, 28, 30, 31, 47, 67, 97, 98, 106, 116, 140, 155, 158, 159, 162, 170
Commuters, 67, 81
Comradeship, *see* Community spirit
Contraception, 79
Cooden, Sussex, 42
Cooking *see* Food
Co-operative movement, 81
Corbett, Harry, 47
Corncrakes, 81
Cot deaths, 78
Country pubs, development of, 54–6
Coventry, 25
Cows, 42, 60, 75, 96, 97, 106, 112, 161
Crapstone, Devon, 122
Cream, 94
Credit, 61, 154
Crewe, 111
Cricket, 13, 31–2, *33*, 37, 39–40, *39*, 134
Crickets, 18, 83
Crickhowell, 62
Crocodiles, 72
Crowhurst, Sussex, 34, 47
Curragh, The, 80
Customs,146–7, 158

Damerell, Joyce, 122–33
Dancing and dance bands, 98–9, *98*, *100*, 125, *125*, 170
Dankworth, Johnny, 30
Dartmoor, 126–33
Darts, 58, *58*
Dawyck Estate, 136
Dean, Oxon ,117
Deaths, sudden, 35–6
Debt, 36
Decimalisation,144–5
De Dion Bouton, 75, *77*
Deer, 106
Dentistry, 72
Development, 7, 26
Devon, 12, 49, 86–109, *96*, *106*, 122–33, *127*
Dialects, 88, 96, 168, 176
Discipline, 145, 161, 176
Disease, *see* Medicine

Dispensing, 77
Ditchley, Oxon, 117
Dixon, Oliver, 125
Doctors, 8, 35, 64, 70, 72–81, *80*, 122, 128, 140, 148, 180
Dodd, Tommy, 27
Dog cart, 23
Dogs, 23, 46, 59, 92, 112, 123, 126, *126*, 132, 148, *149*
Domesday Book, 41
Domestic service, *see* Housemaids
Dominie, 134–45
Donkeys, 18, 97
Door to door sales/deliveries, 27–8, *28*, 64, 71, 144, 151–2
Dorset, 48–60
Dovaston, John, 167
Drabble, Phil, 157
Drainage, 52, 63, 116
Dramatics, amateur, 46, 47, *141*, *180*, 140
Drapers, 62
Drinks, *see also* Meals, 48–60, 91, 94, 126, 162
Drumree, Co Meath, 81
Drunks, 91, 167
Dublin, 80, 81
Dublin, County, 73–5
Ducks, 64, 94, 116
Dunsany, Co Meath, 74–81
Dunsany, Lord, 75, 79–80

East Sussex Foxhounds, 38
Eccentrics, 37–8, 91, 113, 179
Eddleston, Peeblesshire, *136*, *143*, 144–5
Edinburgh University, 135
Education, *see* Schools
Eggs, 65, 94, 160
Egon Ronay, 56
Elections, 134
Electricity, 18, 22, 27, 116, 128, 152
Emergencies, 75, 141
Empire Day, *12*, 21, *22*
Endicott, Bert, 58
Essex, 96, 171–87
Evacuees, 103, *152*
Excise licences, 45
Exmoor, 105–6
Exorcism, 107–8

Factories, 14, 26, 28
Fairless, John, *134*, 134–45
Faith healing, 106–8, 128
Family life, 26, 96
Farming, 16, 60, 61, 64, 72, 75–6, 81, 86–109, 111, 112, 116, 128, 136, 141, 152, 153, 154, 158, 161, 165–6, 171–87
Ferreting, 92
Fetes, 13, 120
Fighting, 70
Fingall, Lord, 75
Fire Brigade, 42
Fires and firewood, 19, 22, 24, 42, 53, 162, 164–5
Fish and fishing, 137, 140, 144, 158
Flats, 28
Fleas, 92, 127
Fletcher, Cyril, 186
Flooding, 143
Flowers, 15, 19, 24, 46, 54, 73, 90, 133, 163
Food, 15, 18, 19, 20, 21, *23*, 24, 27, 47, 56, 61–71, 87–8, 94, 97, 120, 126, 127, *127*, 140, 143, 144, 150–8, 160, 162, 163, 164, 173, 189

Football, 44, 60, 67, 187
Ford, *174*
Foreign Office, 135
Forestry, 136, *165*
Foster children, 105
Foxhunting, 16, 38, *38*, 40, 49, 75–6, 106, 123, 124, 162
Fridges, 67, 152
Fruit, 15, 23, 66, 67, 161, 162, 163, 167
Fruit juices, 54
Fulwell, Oxon, 117
Funerals, 28, 41, 78, 99–100, 109

Gamekeepers, 141, 153, 161, 162, 168
Games, 17, 19, 26, 58, 88–90
Gardens and gardening,15, 22, 24, 35, 37, *37*, 44, *44*, 94, 116, 132, 159–70, *164*, *169*
Geese, 94
George III, King, 50
Ginger beer, 54
Glover, Daisy, 144
Gossips, 110, 158
Great Train Robbery, 177
Greengrocers, 62
Grenfell, Joyce, 30
Grouse, 132
Guides, Girl, 132
Guns, 36, 63, 72, 112, 123, 167, 177, 185
Gwynne, Annie, 64
Gwynne, Eunice, 61–71
Gwynne, John, *61*, 61–71
Gwynne, Leslie, 64
Gwynne, William, *62*, *63*, 64
Gypsies, 67, 82, 110, 126, 154, 168, 177–8, 186–7

Hall and Woodhouse brewery, 52, 53, 54, 60
Hampshire, 171–87
Handcuffs, 45, 183
Hardwick, Earl of, 124
Hares, 65, 132
Hartland, Devon, 86–109, *102*, *103*
Harvest, *82*, 166, 172, *181*
Harvest festivals, 30, 67, 106
Hay, 51, 89, *90*, 91–2, 97, *97*, 134, 160
Heating, *see also* Fires, 87, 116
Hedgehogs, 168
Heritors, 136
Highclere, Hants, 172
Hildenborough, *115*
Hinstock, Shropshire, 110–16
Hogsty End, 15
Holidays, 19, 24–5, 62–3, 70, 87, 99
Holly, 65
Holsworthy, Devon, 96, 102, 104
Home, Gordon, 57
Home Guard, 24
Homes, 8, 12, 17, 28, 64, 81, 94, 101, 111–12, 116, 130, 132, *139*, 144, 151, 162, *174*, 181
Hoops, 19, 21
Horn dance, 158
Hornets, 167, *167*
Horse-racing, 51, 71
Horses, 10–11, 16, 41–2, 49, 53, 67, 72, 75–6, 77, 91, 92, 97, 122, 123, 124–5, 148, 160, 163, 164, 166, 172
Horticultural societies, 134, 174
Hospitals, 64, 67, 74
Houghton, Hants, 181
Hours of work, 23, 25, 35, 43, 112, 116, 117, 143, 163, 165
Housemaids, 14–30, *16*, *26*, 152, 168
Hove, 32

INDEX

Hucksters, 65, 67
Hughes, Reverend Christopher, 126
Humour, 36–7, 41, 140, 145, 161, 179–80, 185–6
Hutchings, Benny, 53
Hypnosis, 86, 103, 107–8, 128

Injuries *see* Accidents
Innerleithen, Borders, 144
Insular communities, 97, 180
Ireland, 72–81, 85
Irish Free State, 66
Ironmonger's, 62
Isle of Wight, 9

Jackdaws, 168, *168*
Jackson, Margaret, 7, *14*, 14–30, *26*, *27*
Jeffrey, Jack, 90
Johnson, Joy, *110*, 110–21
Jones, Harry, 167
Jones, Jean, *170*
Jones, Olive, 168
Jones, Will, *159*, 159–70, *170*

Kelvedon Hatch, Essex ,176–80
Kennedy, President, 47
Kenyon, Col John,170
Kenyon, Lloyd, 161
Killeen, Co Meath, 81
Kilmessan, Co Meath, 74–81
Kilmoon, Co Meath, 74
Kingslang Primary School, Peebles, 135, 141
Kitchener, 47
Knives, 36

Lambs, *see* Sheep
Lancashire, 159–70
Lane, Cleo, 30
Lauderdale, Earl of, 41
Laundry, 160
Lavatories, 47, 116, 159
Laying out of bodies, 128
Leamington Spa, 25
Leather, 150
Lemonade, 54
Letter carriers, 112–13
Lewis, Dick, 167
Librarians, 134
Lice, 127
Lighting, 22, 53, 128, 164
Livestock Register, 179
Lockeridge, Wilts, 125
Lost property 46, 182–3
Lottery, National, 71
Loyalty, 32, 158

Macmillan, Sir Harold, 47
Magistrates, 45, 186
Malnutrition, 78
Marbles, 88
Margaret, Princess, 30
Margarine, 66
Markets, 62, 63, 67, 96, 97, 153, 158, 160, 166, 174
Marlborough Common, Wilts, 127
Marler, Major, 26
Marriages, 27, 74
Matches, 51
Maypoles, 146, *146*
Meals, *see* Food
Meat, *see also* Butchers, 57, 67, 150–8, 162
Meath, County, 72–81
Meath Foxhounds, 75
Medicine, 8, 15, 19, 72–81, 107, 115, 116, 122–33, 134, 148, 170

Mice, 167–8
Midwifery, 76–7, 122–33
Mildmay, Lord, 125
Milk and milkmen, 18, 71, 106, 112, 152
Milton Combe, Devon, 133
Milton Keynes, 26, 28
Mistletoe, 65
Modern conveniences, 106
Moles, 92, 168
Molland, Devon, 105
Montgomery, General, 47
Morris dancing, 84
Mothers' Union, 104, 126
Motorbikes and scooters, 76, *76*, 122, *129*, 144, 182, *186*
Mountbatten, Lord Louis, 182
Mulling boot, *48*, 60

Murnane, Alice, *72*, *73*, *74*, *75*, 72–81, *81*
Murnane, Dr Jack, 74–81
Mushrooms, 65
Music, 21, 58, 98–9, 133, 139

National Health Service, 124, 128
Neighbours, *see* Community spirit
Nether Wallop, Hants, 172
News, 62, 161
Newton Farm, Hartland, 87
Newton, Staffs, 152
Nightingale, John, 180
Ninfield, Sussex, 36
Nissen huts, 132
North Molton, Devon, 105
Notebooks, 44
Nurses and nursing, 72, 111, 122–33, *129*, *130*, *131*

Oddfellows groups, *15*, 26
Official Secrets Act, 119
Old Bull and Bush, 50
Organs, 65, 113–14
Oswestry, 160
Outings, 19–20, 55, 174
Overton, Wilts, 124
Oxfordshire, 110–21, 176
Owls, 158

Palestine police, 32
Parish coal, 12, 17
Parish councils, 12
Park Estate, Dorset, 52
Parsons, F.J., 32, 37, 40, 41
Parties, 21, 145, 161, 164
Partridges, 81, 132, 167, 173
Paxton, Sir Joseph, 23
Payment in kind, 75
Payne, Roland, *29*
Pearl, Margaret,175
Pearl, Peter, *171*, 171–87, *173*, *177*
Peebles High School, 135
Peeblesshire, 134–45
Peel, Sir Robert, 176
Pennington, Dorothy, 101, *104*
Pennington, Reverend Fred, 86–109, *86*, *97*, *98*, *104*

Perchard, Frank, *31*, 31–47, *32*
Perquisites, 137, 153
Pertwee, Jon, 185
Pests, 94, 167–8, 183
Petrol, 62, 76, 80, 125, 141
Pevensey Marshes, 41
Pheasants, 41, 126, 137, 161, 173
Pickles, 94
Pigs, 16, 19, 42, 50, 53, 86, 97, 116, 154, *154*, 157, 158, 160, 161, 162
Pipes, 51, 60, 91
Ploughing, 174
Plover, golden, 81
Plunkett, Edward, 79–80
Plunkett, Horace, 75, 81
Plymouth, 123
Poachers, 168, 176–7, 186–7
Pocket money, 21, 151, 160, 161
Police, 8, 15, 31–47, *34*, *35*, *43*, 46, 53–4, 62, 63, 64, 115–16, 120, 143, 157, 165, 167, 171–87, *183*, *186*
Politics, 40–1, 143–4
Polling stations, 134, 143
Poltergeists, 108
Poole, Dorset, 54
Portman Hunt, 49
Postmen, 9, 17, 26, *112*, *113*, *121*, *163*, 152, 162, 173–4
Post offices, 8, 12, 15, 81, 110–21, *114*,

115, 117, 118, 132, 140, 141, 161
Potatoes, 161, 166
Poteen, 72 , 85
Poverty, 8, 17, 19, 27, 74, 78–9, 126, 127, 128, 155, 162
Pradoe, Shropshire, 159–70, *160*
Pranks, 63
Preserves, 94
Prisoners of war, 173
Public houses, 8, 13, 26, 38–9, 48–60, 62, *51, 52, 57, 58, 59,* 76, 99, 116, 117, 132, 153, 154, 167, 177, 185
Punishment, 147–8

Quizzes, 174

Rabbits, 18, 65, 67, 69, 155, 166, 173
Radio, 24, 30, 34, 57, 140
Rag-and-bone man, 18, *18*
Railways, *see* Trains
Ration books, *71*
Rationing, 25, 71, 73, 76, 121, 125, 155
Rats, 167, 183
Red Cross, 130
Red Lion, Blandford, 51
Refuse collection, 64
Registrars, 134
Remembrance Sunday, 94
Rent, 17, 165–6
Respect, 31–2
Riddles, 85
Roads and roadmen, 12, 27, 36, 41, 49–50, 64, 75, 113, 122, 151, 171
Rochdale, Lancs, 170
Roestown, Dunshaughlin, 81
Rogation Sunday, 114
Romanies, *see* Gypsies
Romsey, Hants, 180–7
Royal Academy, 22
Royal Air Force, 22, 23, 62, 69, 115–16, 154, 172–3
Royal Navy, 50–1
Royal Society for the Protection of Animals, 41, 46, 182
Ruyton-Eleven-Towns, 161, 163

Sacrilege, 45, 184–5
Salary, *see* Wages
Salt, 66
Salvation Army, 58
Samaritans, The, 105, 106
Sand, 97
School, 8, 12, 16, 18, 19, 22, 30, 50, 63, 73, 85, 87, 90, 96, 111, 112, 116, 117, 123, 125, 132, 134–45, *138*, *139*, 151, 152, 155, 161, 162, 172
Scotland, 25
Scouts, Boy, 17, *17*, 132
Security, 120, 160, 182
Selborne, Hants, 82–3
Self-sufficiency, 8, 62, 94, 116, 166
Serfdom, 125, 162, 187
Seventh child, the, 84–5
Sewing, 51, 170
Sheep, 7, 64, 75, *75*, 86, 92, 94, 97, 106, 127, *127*, 168
Shipbourne, *114*
Shipwrecks, 90–1
Shooting, 41, 51, 81, 123, 126, 132, 161, 167
Shops, 6, 8, 12, 20, 21, 61–71, 68–9, 112, 132, 144, 150–8, *156, 188*
Shows, *29*, 41, 46, 132
Shropshire, 110–21, 159–70
Sibley, Jean, 51
Sibley, John, *48*, 48–60, *51, 56*
Singing, 17, 21, 30, 137

Sir Watkin Williams-Wynn's Hounds, 162
Skating, 19
Slaughtering, 16, 121, 153–4, *154*, 155, 157
Smallholdings, 67
Smuggling, 90
Snow, *see* Weather, severe
Somerset, 97
South Africa, 72–4
South Dorset Hunt, 49
South Ockendon, Essex, 176
Speir's School, Beith, 135
Speke's Mill, Devon, 97
Spelsbury, Oxon, 116–21
Squatters' camp, 127
Squirearchy, 12, 32, 49, 113
Staffordshire, 146, 150–8
Staghunting, 75, 106
Stobo, Peeblesshire, *135*, 135–44
Stockbridge, Hants, 184
Stocks, 147–8, *147*
Stoke, Devon, 91, 93
Stone-picking, 171
St Patrick, 85
Stucley, Sir Dennis, 108
Stucley, Sir Lewis, 87
Sturminster Marshall, Dorset, 48–60
Suffolk, 172, 176
Suicides, 8, 21, *21*, 161
Sunday observance, 30, 170
Sunday school, 18, 21, *21*, 161
Superstitions, 78, 84–5, 128, 146–7, 148, 158
Sussex, 31–47
Swanage, 172
Swans, 163–4
Sweets, 67, 172
Swimming, 97, 162

Talbot, Arthur, 41
Talgarth, 61–71, *65, 66*
Tara Hill, Co Meath, 74, 81
Taston, Oxon, 117
Tea, 63–4, 64, 70
Teddy Boys, 53
Tedworth Hunt, 124
Telegrams, 112, 161
Telephones, 45, 117, 140
Television, 43, 46, 59, 185
Thatching, 172
Theatre, 77
Thornbury, Devon, 104
Timber, 64
Tiverton, 103–4
Toads, 24
Tobacco, 51, 53
Tops, 19
Tourists, 70
Tractors, 36, 102, *174, 175, 183*, 186
Trains, 19, 25, *25*, 36, 67, 77, 95, 111, 143, 144, *145*
Tramps, 27, 117, *142*, 142–3, 168
Transport, 8, 23, *34*, 61, 67, 70, 75, 92, 95–6, 97, 122–3, 139, 152, 153, 160, 164, 172
Tring, Herts, 121
Tripe, 150
Truncheons, 44, 53
Turkeys, 75, 94, 95, 153
Turner, Sgt Bert, 41–2
Turnspits, 148, *149*
Tweed, River, 136, 137, 142
Twitchen, Devon, 105

Undertakers, 112, 116, 179–80
Uniform, *see* Clothing

University College Dublin, *74*
Uttoxeter, Staffs, 151, 154, 158

Vagrants, *see* Tramps
Vandals, 45, 46
Vans, 34, 65, 144, 152, 179–80, *185*
Veterinary surgeons, 112, 116
Village decline, 8, 28, 116
Village, definition of, 7
Village employment, 8
Village green, 112
Village halls, 13, *29, 100*, 114, 117, 132, 133, 170
Village organisation, 12, 30, 46, 181
Village populations, 8, 34, 62, 79, 81, 112, 117, 132, 138, 139, 144, 145, 158, 170, 181
Village pride, 45–6
Village sports, 67, 134, 135, 187
Villages, the attraction of, 7–13
Voluntary activities, 46
Voting, 143

Wages, 32, 64, 65, 75, 79, 94, 104, 112, 137, 138, 146, 151, 152, 162, 176, 187
Waggons, *see* Carts
Wakes, 78, *78–9*
Walking, 16, 87, 97, 158, 162, 172, 182
Ward Staghounds, 75
Washing, 22, 152
Water, 63, 116, 120, 143, 152, 154, 165, 172
Wavendon, Bucks, 14–30, *21, 22, 30*
Weale, Tom, 63
Weather, severe, 19, 22, 27, 47, 63, 71, 75, 80, 83, 96, 106, 120, 122, 127, 139, 141, *154*, 155, 187
Weddings, 32
Weekenders, 67
Wells, *152*
Welsh cakes, 69
Welsh-English friction, 168
Welsh language, 65, 71
West Felton, Shrops, 116, 160, 170
Westward Ho!, Devon, 101
Weymouth, Dorset, 50
Whaddon Chase Hunt, 16
Whipping, 147–8
Whistles, 44
Wilde, Oscar, 37
Williams, Elizabeth, *110*, 110–21
Wilson, Victor, *150*, 150–8, *153*
Wiltshire, 122–33
Wimborne, Dorset, 50, 59
Winchester, Marquis of, 172
Wine, 34, 54, 71, 126, 170
Woburn Sands, 15, 19, 24
Woodhouse, Brigadier, 52
Woodhouse, Edward, 60
Woolsery, Devon, *106*, 109
Woolworth's, 19
Women's Institute, 12, 132
Worcestershire, 116
Workhouses, 168
World War I, 17, 47, 69, 75, 91–2, 94, 96, 161
World War II, 24–5, 26, 30, 33, 46, 53, 54, 62, 69, 76, 80, 103, 115, 116, 120–1, 125, 127, 134, 154–5, 170, 172–3
Worsley, Reverend, 104
Wrens, 25
Wright, Lady Jimmy, 124

Yelverton, Devon, 122
Youth clubs, 67